First World War
and Army of Occupation
War Diary
France, Belgium and Germany

4 DIVISION
10 Infantry Brigade
Household Battalion
6 November 1916 - 15 February 1918

WO95/1481/1

The Naval & Military Press Ltd
www.nmarchive.com
Published in association with The National Archives

Published by

The Naval & Military Press Ltd

Unit 10 Ridgewood Industrial Park,

Uckfield, East Sussex,

TN22 5QE England

Tel: +44 (0) 1825 749494

www.naval-military-press.com

www.nmarchive.com

This diary has been reprinted in facsimile from the original. Any imperfections are inevitably reproduced and the quality may fall short of modern type and cartographic standards.

Contents

Document type	Place/Title	Date From	Date To
Heading	10 Infantry Brigade. Household Battalion. 1916 Nov to 1918 Feb. 7 Bn Argyll & Sutherland Highlanders. 1914 Dec to 1916 Feb. 2 Bn Duke of Wellingtons Regiment 1918 Jan to 1919 June. 2 Bn Royal Dublin Fusiliers 1914 Aug to 1916 Nov.		
Heading	4th Division Household Battn 10th Bde November & December 1916		
Heading	10th Brigade 4th Division Battalion arrived Havre from U.K. 10.11.16 & joined 10th Brigade; 4th Division The Household Battalion November 1916		
War Diary	London	06/11/1916	08/11/1916
War Diary	Southampton	09/11/1916	09/11/1916
War Diary	Havre	10/11/1916	10/11/1916
War Diary	Le Havre	11/11/1916	11/11/1916
War Diary	Gamaches	12/11/1916	17/11/1916
War Diary	Rogeant	18/11/1916	30/11/1916
Heading	10th Brigade 4th Division The Household Battalion December 1916		
Heading	War Diary of Household Battalion Period 1st December To 31st December 1916 Volume 2		
War Diary	Toeufles	01/12/1916	03/12/1916
War Diary	Vaux	04/12/1916	04/12/1916
War Diary	Camp 112	05/12/1916	20/12/1916
War Diary	Camp 107	21/12/1916	23/12/1916
War Diary	U20.b.8.9 Combles 1/10,000 IV Div Provl Map 1/10,000	23/12/1916	24/12/1916
War Diary	U.14c.1.2 Combles 1/10,000	25/12/1916	27/12/1916
War Diary	Camp X Maurepas Halte	28/12/1916	30/12/1916
War Diary	Camp 112	31/12/1916	31/12/1916
Heading	4th Division War Diaries 10th Infantry Bde Household Battn January to June 1917		
Heading	War Diary of Household Battalion From 1st January 1917 To 31st January 1917 Vol 3		
War Diary	Camp 112	01/01/1917	18/01/1917
War Diary	C 21 C 1.7 C 26 A.9.5 Ref 1/10,000 French Map 57c NW 4 Bouchavesnes	18/01/1917	23/01/1917
War Diary	Suzanne	23/01/1917	24/01/1917
War Diary	Neuville Les Bray	25/01/1917	27/01/1917
War Diary	Camp K 22 C Central 1/40000 Albert	28/01/1917	30/01/1917
War Diary	Camp 13	31/01/1917	31/01/1917
Heading	War Diary of Household Battalion From 4th February 1917 To 3rd March 1917 Vol4		
War Diary	Camp 13	01/02/1917	02/02/1917
War Diary	Bray Sur Somme	02/02/1917	08/02/1917
War Diary	Bray Camp 17 N. of Suzanne	09/02/1917	10/02/1917
War Diary	Asquith Flats B16 d8.2	10/02/1917	12/02/1917
War Diary	Asquith Flats	12/02/1917	14/02/1917
War Diary	Aldershot Map Of C8d 3.05.7 Bouchavesnes 1/10,000	15/02/1917	16/02/1917
War Diary	Aldershot	16/02/1917	21/02/1917
War Diary	Camp13 K 22.C Central Albert 1/40,000	22/02/1917	03/03/1917

War Diary	Corbie	04/03/1917	04/03/1917
War Diary	Bertangles D/1 Ref Amiens Sh 17,/100,000	05/03/1917	05/03/1917
War Diary	Beauval D/5 Ref Lens 1/100,000	06/03/1917	06/03/1917
War Diary	Villers L'Hopital C/4 Lens 1/100,000	07/03/1917	10/03/1917
War Diary	Villers L'Hopital	11/03/1917	11/03/1917
War Diary	Petit Bouret Sur Canche G 33 Sh 51c 1/40,000	12/03/1917	12/03/1917
War Diary	Petit Bouret Sur Canche G Hr 3.8 Central France Sheet 51c 1/40,000	13/03/1917	13/03/1917
War Diary	Savy D.4.d.7.6	14/03/1917	14/03/1917
War Diary	Laresset K.5.c.8.5	15/03/1917	15/03/1917
War Diary	Maroeuil F 27.c.3.5	16/03/1917	23/03/1917
War Diary	Savy	24/03/1917	24/03/1917
War Diary	Camblain Chatelain I 9 T19 1/40,000	25/03/1917	31/03/1917
Heading	War Diary of Household Battalion From 1st April 1917 To 30th April 1917 Volume 6		
War Diary	Camblain Chatelain I.9.d Sheet 36 B 1/40.000	01/04/1917	07/04/1917
War Diary	Frevillers V.1 Central Sheet 36 B 1/40,000	08/04/1917	08/04/1917
War Diary	X Hutment F 19.a.5.7 51c 1/40,000	09/04/1917	09/04/1917
War Diary	Amzim St Aubin T Blue Line H.7.d.85 Trench Map	09/04/1917	13/04/1917
War Diary	Blue Line H.7.d 85 Trench Map	14/04/1917	16/04/1917
War Diary	Black Line G.12.a 7b Trench Map	16/04/1917	17/04/1917
War Diary	H.11.b.6.2 Trench Map 51b NW 1/20,000	17/04/1917	30/04/1917
Miscellaneous	Household Battn Preliminary Instruction.1	03/04/1917	03/04/1917
Miscellaneous	Preliminary Instructions No.2		
Miscellaneous	Preliminary Instructions No.4		
Map			
Miscellaneous	Appendix "B" Position of Headquarters Dumps Etc		
Operation(al) Order(s)	10th Infantry Brigade Operation Order No.15	05/04/1917	05/04/1917
Miscellaneous	March Table To Accompany 10th Inf. Brigade Operation Order No.15		
Operation(al) Order(s)	10th Infantry Brigade Operation Order No.17	06/04/1917	06/04/1917
Miscellaneous	March Table To Accompany 10th Brigade Operation Order No.17		
Miscellaneous	Narration of Operations of Household Battn 11/4/17-12/4/17	12/04/1917	12/04/1917
Operation(al) Order(s)	10th Infantry Bde O.O No. 18	11/04/1917	11/04/1917
Operation(al) Order(s)	10th Infy Bde Operation Order No.19	13/04/1917	13/04/1917
Miscellaneous	Messages And Signals		
Operation(al) Order(s)	10th Infantry Brigade Operation Order No.22	20/04/1917	20/04/1917
Miscellaneous	March Table To Accompany 10th Inf. Bde Operation Order No.22		
Heading	War Diary of Household Battalion For Month Of May 1917 Volume 7		
War Diary		01/05/1917	31/05/1917
Miscellaneous	Household Battalion List of Awards		
Operation(al) Order(s)	10th Inf. Bde. O.O No.28	02/05/1917	02/05/1917
Miscellaneous	Time Table Of Trench		
Miscellaneous	A Form Messages And Signals		
Miscellaneous	Household Battn Narrative of Operations	15/05/1917	15/05/1917
Miscellaneous	A Form Messages And Signals		
Miscellaneous	10th Bde Preliminary Inst No.1	09/05/1917	09/05/1917
Miscellaneous	Household Battalion Narrative of Operations May 11th/12th	16/05/1917	16/05/1917
Heading	War Diary of Houschold Battalion From 1st June 1917 To 30th June 1917 Volume 8		
Miscellaneous	Household Battalion List of Awards		

War Diary	Houvin Hovigneul	01/06/1917	12/06/1917
War Diary	Arras	12/06/1917	15/06/1917
War Diary	Balmoral Camp E 18 A 2.8 Ref Sh Arras 1/10,000	16/06/1917	18/06/1917
War Diary	Ref Sh Plouvain 1/10000	18/06/1917	18/06/1917
War Diary	Balmoral Camp	19/06/1917	23/06/1917
War Diary	Front Line Left Sub-Sector	23/06/1917	27/06/1917
War Diary	Stirling Camp H 13d 75 Ref Sh 51b NW 1/20,000	27/06/1917	30/06/1917
Miscellaneous	Appendix I		
Map	Map		
Miscellaneous	Appendix II		
Heading	4th Division War Diaries 10th Infantry Bde Household Battn 1917 July-1918 Feb		
Heading	War Diary of Household Battalion From 1st July 1917 To 31st July 1917 Volume 9		
War Diary	Stirling Camp H 13d 75 Ref Sh 51b NW 1/20,000	01/07/1917	05/07/1917
War Diary	Railway Cutting H 23a D E	05/07/1917	11/07/1917
War Diary	10th Brigade Sector Lines before Roeux	11/07/1917	12/07/1917
War Diary	Line Before Roeux	13/07/1917	16/07/1917
Miscellaneous	A Form Messages And Signals		
War Diary	Lines Before Roeux	16/07/1917	20/07/1917
War Diary	Stirling Camp	21/07/1917	31/07/1917
Miscellaneous	Appendix B	17/07/1917	17/07/1917
Heading	Household Battalion War Diary Volume 10		
War Diary		31/07/1917	07/08/1917
War Diary	Cutting H 23a D C	08/08/1917	15/08/1917
War Diary	Stirling Camp H 13d 5.5	08/08/1917	15/08/1917
War Diary	Stirling Camp	16/08/1917	18/08/1917
War Diary	Crete Trch	18/08/1917	26/08/1917
War Diary	Stirling Camp	27/08/1917	31/08/1917
Heading	War Diary of Household Battalion From 6th November 1916 To 30th November 1916 Volume No.1		
Heading	Household Battalion War Diary Volume 11 From September 1st To September 30th 1917		
Map	Map		
War Diary	Stirling Camp	01/09/1917	02/09/1917
War Diary	Crete Tr	03/09/1917	06/09/1917
War Diary	Arras	07/09/1917	18/09/1917
War Diary	Bailleulval Proven	19/09/1917	28/09/1917
War Diary	Proven	29/09/1917	30/09/1917
War Diary	Soult Camp		
Heading	War Diary of Household Battalion From 1st October 1917 To 31st October 1917 Volume 12		
War Diary	Soult Camp Ref Sh 28 N.W. 1/20,000 B 23 A.2.3	01/10/1917	04/10/1917
War Diary	Iron Cross C 3.a.8.6	04/10/1917	04/10/1917
War Diary	Au Bongite U 29 d 1.9 Ref Sh Langenark 1/10,000	05/10/1917	06/10/1917
War Diary	Leipsig Camp B 23a 8.1 Ref Sh 28 NW 1/20,000	07/10/1917	08/10/1917
War Diary	Jolie Farm Ref Sh Langemark C 9a 1.8	08/10/1917	09/10/1917
War Diary	Bird Ho U29b 0.3 Jolie FM	09/10/1917	09/10/1917
War Diary	Front Line Right Battn 12th Brigade	10/10/1917	10/10/1917
War Diary	Front Line Right Battn 12th Brigade Ref Sh Broembeek 1/10,000	10/10/1917	12/10/1917
War Diary	Leipsig Camp	13/10/1917	13/10/1917
War Diary	Paddock Wood Camp E 4d 49 Ref Sh 27 1/40000	14/10/1917	14/10/1917
War Diary	St Janter Biezen L 2 B 1.5	15/10/1917	16/10/1917
War Diary	St Janter Biezen	17/10/1917	17/10/1917
War Diary	Duisans	18/10/1917	22/10/1917

War Diary	Schramm Barracks Arras	23/10/1917	24/10/1917
War Diary	College Communale Arras	25/10/1917	31/10/1917
Miscellaneous	Summary Of The Household Battalion From Oct 14th		
Miscellaneous	Appendix 'A'	11/10/1917	11/10/1917
Map	Map		
Miscellaneous	Sketch Map		
Miscellaneous			
Miscellaneous	Appendix "B"		
Miscellaneous	Appendix "A"		
Heading	War Diary of Household Battalion From 1st November 1917 To 30th November 1917 Volume 13		
War Diary	College Communale Arras	01/11/1917	01/11/1917
War Diary	Front Line Cambrai Road Sector O 14a 6.7 O 8b 2.1 (Ref Sh 51b S.W 1/20,000)	01/11/1917	05/11/1917
War Diary	Les Fosses Farm N 11 B9.4 (Ref Sh 51b S.W 1/20,000)	06/11/1917	09/11/1917
War Diary	Brown Line N.10.a	10/11/1917	12/11/1917
War Diary	Brown Line	13/11/1917	16/11/1917
War Diary	Front Line Cambrai Road Sector O.14.a.6.7 O.8.b.2.1 Ref Sheet 51b S.W 1/20,000	17/11/1917	17/11/1917
War Diary	Front Line	18/11/1917	21/11/1917
War Diary	Les Fosses Farm	22/11/1917	25/11/1917
War Diary	College Communale Arras	26/11/1917	27/11/1917
War Diary	College Communale and Bois Des Boeufs N.2.a	28/11/1917	30/11/1917
War Diary	Bois Des Boeufs Camp	30/11/1917	30/11/1917
Heading	War Diary of Household Battalion From 1st December 1917 To 31st December 1917 Volume 14		
War Diary	Bois Des Boeufs	01/12/1917	02/12/1917
War Diary	College Communale Arras	02/12/1917	09/12/1917
War Diary	Right Subsection 10th Bde Front E. Of Monchy Le Preux	10/12/1917	10/12/1917
War Diary	Front Line E Of Monchy Le Preux	11/12/1917	14/12/1917
War Diary	Monchy Defences	14/12/1917	17/12/1917
War Diary	Front Line E Of Monchy	18/12/1917	21/12/1917
War Diary	Wilderness Camp H.31.a.9.3 (51b NW 1/20,000)	22/12/1917	25/12/1917
War Diary	Schramm Barracks Arras	26/12/1917	30/12/1917
War Diary	Wilderness Camp	30/12/1917	31/12/1917
Heading	4th Division Household Battn Disbanded 15th Feb January Bat February 1918		
Heading	War Diary of Household Battalion From 1st January 1918 To 31st January 1918 Volume 15		
War Diary	Wilderness Camp H.31.a9.3 (51b NW 1/20,000)	01/01/1918	06/01/1918
War Diary	Cambrai Road Sector	07/01/1918	07/01/1918
War Diary	Brigade Support Les Fosses Farm	08/01/1918	10/01/1918
War Diary	Cambrai Road Sector	11/01/1918	15/01/1918
War Diary	Brown Line Brigade Reserve	16/01/1918	18/01/1918
War Diary	Schramm Barracks Arras	19/01/1918	23/01/1918
War Diary	Wilderness Camp	23/01/1918	27/01/1918
War Diary	Front Line	27/01/1918	31/01/1918
Heading	War Diary of Household Battalion From 1st February 1918 Until Date Of Disbandment 15 February 1918 Volume 16		
War Diary	Right Front Battalion in Monchy Sector Circle Trench and Support Battn in Curb Switch South	01/02/1918	06/02/1918
War Diary	College Communale Arras	07/02/1918	10/02/1918
War Diary	Arras	11/02/1918	15/02/1918

10 INFANTRY BRIGADE.

HOUSEHOLD BATTALION.

1916 NOV TO 1918 FEB.

7 BN ARGYLL & SUTHERLAND HIGHLANDERS.

1914 DEC TO 1916 FEB.

2 BN DUKE OF WELLINGTONS REGIMENT

1918 JAN TO 1919 JUNE.

2 BN ROYAL DUBLIN FUSILIERS.

1914 AUG TO 1916 NOV.

1481

4th Division.

Household Battn

10th Bde

November + December

1916

FROM UK

10th Brigade.

4th Division.

Battalion arrived HAVRE from U.K. 10.11.16 & joined 10th Brigade; 4th Division.

THE HOUSEHOLD BATTALION

NOVEMBER 1 9 1 6

Army Form C. 2118.

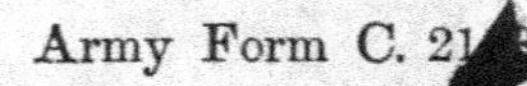

Instructions regarding War Diaries and Intelligence Summaries are contained in F. S. Regs., Part II. and the Staff Manual respectively. Title Pages will be prepared in manuscript.

WAR DIARY
or
INTELLIGENCE SUMMARY

(Erase heading not required.)

Place	Date	Hour	Summary of Events and Information	Remarks and references to Appendices
LONDON.	6.11	1915	Orders received from Headquarters London District for the Battn to embark	
"	7.11	1915	Day spent in preparations for Embarkation.	
	8th		Battalion paraded 8.45 AM. Left Waterloo in 3 Trains for SOUTHAMPTON. Major General Sir Francis Lloyd was present to see departure of the first train.	
			20 Officers & 658 men under Major Earl of Kilmorey embarked on Mona's Queen at 9 P.m. They arrived at HAVRE at 7 A.M. on the 9th & marched to the rest Camp where they awaited the remainder of the Battn.	
SOUTHAMPTON	9th		Remainder of Battalion under Lt Colonel G R Pretal (Strength 12 officers, 302 men) & all the Transport embarked on the AUSTRALIND at 5 PM	
HAVRE.	10th		Arrived at HAVRE. Disembarked at 9 AM. Marched to the Rest Camp & joined the remainder of the Battalion.	[illegible signature]

2449 Wt. W14957/M90 750,000 1/16 J.B.C. & A. Forms/C.2118/12.

Instructions regarding War Diaries and Intelligence Summaries are contained in F. S. Regs., Part II. and the Staff Manual respectively. Title Pages will be prepared in manuscript.

WAR DIARY
or
~~INTELLIGENCE SUMMARY~~
(Erase heading not required.)

Army Form C. 2118.

Place	Date	Hour	Summary of Events and Information	Remarks and references to Appendices
LE HAVRE	11-	11.16	Preparations for proceeding up the line. Orders received from D.A.Q.M.G. Havre Base to entrain at 11.45 P.M. The Battalion paraded at 9.45 P.M & marched to the Gare des Marchandises. Entrainment took 5 hours owing to miscalculation of the Railway officials about our numbers	
GAMACHES	12	11.16	~~Reach~~ Reached our detraining Station, LANGROY GAMACHES at 3.30 P.M. Marched 22 Kilometres to BERNAPRÉ. No 1 Company & H.Q were billeted at BERNAPRÉ the remainder of the Battn at SENARPONT. Arrived at our billets at 9.30 P.M.	
	13	11.16	Resting	
	14	11.16	Company Training. Lieut R. W. Oliver & party of N.C.O's & men marched to TOEUFLES to take over Billets from the Royal Dublin Fusiliers. Brig-Gen Wilding, G.O.C 10th Infantry Brigade, our Brigadier came over to see us	

[illegible signature]

2449 Wt. W14957/M90 750,000 1/16 J.B.C. & A. Forms/C.2118/12.

Instructions regarding War Diaries and Intelligence Summaries are contained in F. S. Regs., Part II. and the Staff Manual respectively. Title Pages will be prepared in manuscript.

WAR DIARY
or
~~INTELLIGENCE SUMMARY~~
(Erase heading not required.)

Army Form C. 2118.

Place	Date	Hour	Summary of Events and Information	Remarks and references to Appendices
GAMACHES	15	11.16	Company Training	
	16	11.16		
	17	11.16	Battalion paraded at 7.30 AM & proceeded to billets round TOEUFLES. Route R of REDERIE, OISEMONT, L of CERISY, St MAXENT-EN-VIMEU, GREBAULT-MESNIL, ERCOURT-TOEUFLES (1/100,000 ABBEVILLE Sheet 14). Arrived 2 PM. H.Q. at ROGEANT. No 1, 2 & 4 Coys at TOEUFLES. No 3 Company at ERCOURT. 2nd Lieut R.W.G. Dill admitted to 12th Field Ambulance	
ROGEANT	18	11.16	Resting	
	20	11.16	Company Training. Captain E.M.S. Mackinty admitted to 12th Field Ambulance. Capt J.H.M. Kirkwood joined the Battn.	
	21, 22, 23	11.16	Company Training	
	24	11.16	Battn inspected by Major-Gen. Hon. W. Lambton, G.O.C. 4th Division. Capt P. Malcolm (Gren Gds) & Capt. W Tobin joined the Battn.	[illegible] Capt & Adjt

2449 Wt. W14957/M90 750,000 1/16 J.B.C. & A. Forms/C.2118/12.

Army Form C. 2118.

Instructions regarding War Diaries and Intelligence Summaries are contained in F. S. Regs., Part II. and the Staff Manual respectively. Title Pages will be prepared in manuscript.

WAR DIARY
or
INTELLIGENCE SUMMARY
(Erase heading not required.)

Place	Date	Hour	Summary of Events and Information	Remarks and references to Appendices
	26	11.16	Party of 100 men under Major Earl of Kilmorey paraded at Bde H.Q. on occasion of presentation of medals to men of 10th Infantry Bde by Major Gen. Hon W. Lambton G.O.C. 4th Division.	
	27	11.16	Battalion Training	
	28	11.16		
	29	11.16		
	30	11.16	Battalion Scheme. Major Gen. Hon W. Lambton & Brig. Gen Wilding attended. Batt. Bayonet fighting team was 2nd in 10th Brigade. Beaten by 2nd Seaforths.	

Hawley [illegible]
Capt & Adjt

2449 Wt. W14957/M90 750,000 1/16 J.B.C. & A. Forms/C.2118/12.

10th Brigade.

4th Division.

THE HOUSEHOLD BATTALION

DECEMBER 1 9 1 6

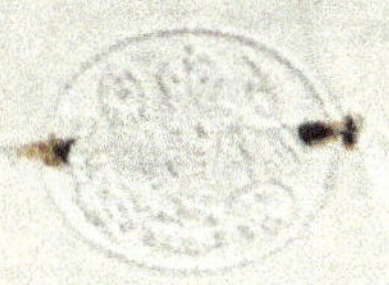

CONFIDENTIAL-

WAR DIARY of HOUSEHOLD BATTALION.

Period:- 1st December to 31st December, 1916.

Volume 2.

W. Hobson Capt
for Captain.
Commanding Household Battalion.

4/1/17.

Vol II

Instructions regarding War Diaries and Intelligence Summaries are contained in F. S. Regs., Part II. and the Staff Manual respectively. Title Pages will be prepared in manuscript.

WAR DIARY
or
~~INTELLIGENCE SUMMARY~~

(Erase heading not required.)

Army Form C. 2118.

Place	Date	Hour	Summary of Events and Information	Remarks and references to Appendices
	1.12.16		Nothing to report.	
TOEUFLES	2.12.16		Our last day at TOEUFLES. Orders for the move arrived.	
	3		Parade 8 AM. Marched via ERCOURT & GREBAULT-MESNIL to OISEMONT where we entrained at 6.45 PM after a wait of over 7 hours. Detrained at MERICOURT at 1.45 AM & marched to our billets at VAUX-SUR-SOMME where we arrived at 4 AM.	
VAUX.	4		Parade 11 AM. Marched via BRAY to Camp 112 (Fork Tree Camp) about 2 km N of BRAY.	
Camp 112	5		2nd Lieut. G.C. NELSON joined the Battalion.	
"	6.		Parade 6.45 AM. Marched by Road Junction N of BRAY along main MARICOURT road to Camp 107 in BRILLON Wood. Captain H.M. Seton-Karr went sick.	
	7		Marched to Camp 20 (Ref. ALBERT 1/40000 A 27 c) which we took over from the Essex Regiment.	

[signature]

2449 Wt. W14957/M90 750,000 1/16 J.B.C. & A. Forms/C.2118/12.

Instructions regarding War Diaries and Intelligence Summaries are contained in F. S. Regs., Part II. and the Staff Manual respectively. Title Pages will be prepared in manuscript.

Army Form C. 2118.

WAR DIARY
or
~~INTELLIGENCE SUMMARY~~

(Erase heading not required.)

Place	Date	Hour	Summary of Events and Information	Remarks and references to Appendices
	10.12.16		Relieved the Warwicks in the right sub-sector U 20 c 7.5 – U 26 A 4.5. A very difficult relief owing to the state of the ground & the late arrival of the guides. No. 1 Coy held the left front line, No. 2 Coy Right front line No. 3 Coy in support & No. 4 Company in reserve. No. 1 Coy's guides led them in the wrong way with the result that their road was blocked. They were fairly heavily shelled on their way in and several men of No. 1 Platoon. The Company got into its position by 1.30 am but 40 of their men were stuck in the mud on the way up, however they were all dug-out before it got light. During the night orders were received that on the night of the 11th the Household Battalion was to relieve the 1st Batt. of the Queen's who were on the right. The Seaforths were to take over the line held by our left front Company.	COMBLES 57C S.W. 1/20,000 Stanley Capt.

2449 Wt. W14957/M90 750,000 1/16 J.B.C. & A. Forms/C.2118/12.

Instructions regarding War Diaries and Intelligence Summaries are contained in F. S. Regs., Part II. and the Staff Manual respectively. Title Pages will be prepared in manuscript.

WAR DIARY
or
INTELLIGENCE SUMMARY
(Erase heading not required.)

Army Form C. 2118.

Place	Date	Hour	Summary of Events and Information	Remarks and references to Appendices
	8.		4th Division relieved a portion of the French XX Corps on the front approximately between U 25 b 5.5 & the Sunken road (inclusive) N of SAILLISEL at U 14 b 9.8. Battalion paraded at 11 AM & marched via MARICOURT, HARDECOURT, MAUREPAS, COMBLES to PRIEZ farm where we were in Brigade reserve. We relieved the 1st Bn ZOUAVES & part of a French Working Battalion. A carrying party of 100 men under Capt Fothe was found for the Warwicks. Casualty 1 man wounded. The Company Commanders & the Signalling Officer spent the night in the trenches with the Warwicks.	COMBLES 57C S.W. 1/20,000
	9.		The Colonel & Adjutant went up to the Headquarters of the Warwicks situated in NEGOTIN trench.	

Stanley
Capt & Adjt

2449 Wt. W14957/M90 750,000 1/16 J.B.C. & A. Forms/C.2118/12.

Instructions regarding War Diaries and Intelligence Summaries are contained in F. S. Regs., Part II. and the Staff Manual respectively. Title Pages will be prepared in manuscript.

WAR DIARY
or
~~INTELLIGENCE SUMMARY~~

(Erase heading not required.)

Army Form C. 2118.

Place	Date	Hour	Summary of Events and Information	Remarks and references to Appendices
	10.12.16		our new left would be the left of the original right front Coy	
	11.		The Brigadier & Brigade Major came up in the morning to discuss the new move. No 2 Company sidestepped to the right & took over the line of the left front company of the Fusiliers, while they held their own original line by posts. No 4 Coy dribbled back to PRIEZ farm where they were to wait till dark & then relieve the right front company of the Fusiliers. ~~The relief of No 1 2 & 3 C~~ No 3 Coy was in support Battalion HQ at RANCOURT & No 1 Coy in reserve near Battn HQ. The relief of No 1. 2 & 3 Companies went off but a large number of No 4 Coy got stuck on their way up & were not dug out till daylight of the 12th.	
	12		During the day the men had a very rough time as it was almost impossible to move owing to the mud. The Brigadier & Col Foster, commanding the Warwicks, came	[illegible] Capt

2449 Wt. W14957/M90 750,000 1/16 J.B.C. & A. Forms/C.2118/12.

Instructions regarding War Diaries and Intelligence Summaries are contained in F. S. Regs., Part II. and the Staff Manual respectively. Title Pages will be prepared in manuscript.

WAR DIARY
or
~~INTELLIGENCE SUMMARY~~
(Erase heading not required.)

Army Form C. 2118.

Place	Date	Hour	Summary of Events and Information	Remarks and references to Appendices
			to Battn. HQ to talk over the situation. It was then decided that the Right Company frontage should be held by posts & that the more exhausted men should be sent back in motor-busses to Camp 16. This was carried out during the night of Dec 12/13	
	13		The Battalion was relieved by 1st Battn. R. Warwickshire Regiment & went into Brigade Reserve at PRIEZ farm. A most successful relief which was complete by 7 p.m. The casualties during these 3 days in the trenches have been. Officers: Wounded. 2/Lieut. H. Brooke Sick. Major Earl of Kilmorey O.R.: Killed 2 ~~Wounded~~ Wounded. 18	
			Capt.	

2449 Wt. W14957/M90 750,000 1/16 J.B.C. & A. Forms/C.2118/12.

Army Form C. 2118.

WAR DIARY
or
~~INTELLIGENCE SUMMARY~~
(Erase heading not required.)

Instructions regarding War Diaries and Intelligence Summaries are contained in F. S. Regs., Part II. and the Staff Manual respectively. Title Pages will be prepared in manuscript.

Place	Date	Hour	Summary of Events and Information	Remarks and references to Appendices
	14		Brigade Reserve at PRIEZ FARM. 7 officers were sent to Hospital. Lieuts. F Haggie. R.C. Chilton 2nd Lieuts B Greenhill. B.L. Gibbs. J Nelson W. Sparkes.	
	15		Major Gen. Hon W. Lambton G.O.C. 4th Division came over in the morning. The Battalion paraded at 2 am & marched via COMBLES to MAUREPAS where they got into motor lorries which took them to BRONFAY FARM. The Battn. then went into Divisional Reserve in Camp 107.	
	16 17 18 19		Nothing of importance to record. The time was spent in refitting & reorganising.	
	20		Mr Campbell went to Hospital	

Stanley [illegible]

2449 Wt. W14957/M90 750,000 1/16 J.B.C. & A. Forms/C.2118/12.

Army Form C. 2118.

WAR DIARY
or
~~INTELLIGENCE SUMMARY~~
(Erase heading not required.)

Instructions regarding War Diaries and Intelligence Summaries are contained in F. S. Regs., Part II. and the Staff Manual respectively. Title Pages will be prepared in manuscript.

Place	Date	Hour	Summary of Events and Information	Remarks and references to Appendices
Camp 107	21.12.16		Work of refitting continued. Capt. Kirkwood & Mr. Sanford went up to the new line in the Evening to get full particulars of the situation from the Essex Regt., in view of the relief to take place on the 23rd inst.	MAPS. ALBERT 1/40,000 COMBLES 1/10,000 IV Div. Prov. map. 1/10,000.
	22.12.16		One officer per Coy went up to the trenches to take over their respective line of trench, and await the arrival of their units, as any communication between the front or support trenches & the reserve trench by daylight was impossible. The Battn spent the day in completing its equipment, & remobilizing generally.	
	23.12.16.		Lt. Col. W. R. Portal went to Hospital and the Battn was temporarily commanded by Capt. John Kirkwood. The Battn moved out of Camp 107 at 10-30 AM and were served with a hot meal at F24 c 6.4 (ALBERT 1/40,000) before embussing there at 1pm. Battn disembussed at MAUREPAS and proceeded to FREGICOURT X Rds — Each platoon moving off independently, 5 minutes interval between platoons, & one quarter of an hour between Companies — at FREGICOURT X Rds guides from the Essex Regt. met them and took them to their different Sectors. The relief was completed at 7-45 pm. The dispositions were as follows. Two Companies in the front line, each of 3 platoons with a total strength of Eighty men Each.	John Kirkwood Capt.

2449 Wt. W14957/M90 750,000 1/16 J.B.C. & A. Forms/C.2118/12.

Army Form C. 2118.

Instructions regarding War Diaries and Intelligence Summaries are contained in F. S. Regs., Part II. and the Staff Manual respectively. Title Pages will be prepared in manuscript.

WAR DIARY
or
~~INTELLIGENCE~~ SUMMARY

(Erase heading not required.)

Place	Date	Hour	Summary of Events and Information	Remarks and references to Appendices
U 20.b.8.9 COMBLES 1/10,000. IV DIV PROVL MAP 1/10,000	23.12.16		These two Coys were furnished by No 4 Coy under Capt Malcolm on the right, & No 3 Coy under Capt Pelly, on the left. The right Coy had five posts and three Lewis guns, as well as three Brigade MG's - their right was in touch with the 11th Bde (Somerset L.I). The left Coy comprised eight posts including three Lewis guns, & one bombing post. There was one Bde MG in ~~this~~ sector - Their left Platoon was in touch with the Seaforth Highlanders in SAILLY-SAILLISEL. The whole of this front line trench was in a very broken down condition & in many places completely cut off from direct communication - it was, also, in many places full of water, & could, therefore only be held by posts. There was very little wire out in front, & what there was was only plain French wire. The German trench line varied from 20 yds distance on the left to about 200 yds on the right. The whole area ~~included was~~ from U.14.d 9.7 on the left to BERLIN Tr (which could not be identified) on the right. The Support trench was situated in BREAD Tr. and was held by 50 men of No I Coy under Mr Olivier. There were 3 Lewis ~~Maxim~~ guns in this line, and one Bde MG a few yards away from the left flank. There was no direct communication between this trench and the front line when we took over, as the communication trenches had either tumbled in or were filled with water. The Battn H.Q were close behind the support trench, & in another dug-out close by the advance dressing station & stretcher bearers were established. About 100 yds in rear, close to the junction of BULLY & BREAD Trs, the Battn dump was situated, and the reserve trench, which was held by the remaining half of No I Coy (under Mr Portal) was situated to the N. of BULLET XRds along the BAPAUME ROAD.	M. Kennard Capt

Army Form C. 2118.

WAR DIARY
or
~~INTELLIGENCE SUMMARY~~
(Erase heading not required.)

Instructions regarding War Diaries and Intelligence Summaries are contained in F. S. Regs., Part II. and the Staff Manual respectively. Title Pages will be prepared in manuscript.

Place	Date	Hour	Summary of Events and Information	Remarks and references to Appendices
V. 20 b 8.9 COMBLES 1/10,000 IV DIV Prov[l] MAP 1/10,000.	23.12.16		The Bg[de] dump was situated about 500 yds E of the FREGICOURT XR[ds] - here there was a permanent carrying party of fifty men of No 2 Coy under Capt. Tobin. The Reg[tl] aid station under our M.O was also at this spot. Several officers from the front, support and reserve trenches remained in relief at COMBLES, as well as the remainder of Nos 3 & 4 Coys who were placed in charge of Mr Bridgeman.	
			Capt. Kirkwood and Capt. Lord Stanley went round the front line trenches during the night. It was impossible to visit the various posts except by walking along the top of the trench line.	
	24.12.16		The situation generally speaking was quiet. The enemy were not visible but appeared to be improving their trenches, from what could be seen of the mud being thrown out of their trench line.	
			There was a certain amount of intermittent shelling on both sides, but was not in either case directed against the front line trenches.	
			During the night a certain amount of wire & other material had been carried up from the Bg[de] to the Batt[n] dump & work had been commenced by improving shelters, re-claiming trenches, digging latrines, and the support Coy commenced digging a Communication trench from their line to the front line trenches.	
			Two men of No. 2 Coy were killed by a shell at the dump.	
			Capt. Kirkwood visited the front line at night.	Wm Kirkwood Capt.
			Batt[n] HQ moved back to a dug-out in the reserve trench. and the O.C No 2 Coy took over the HQ dug-out	

2449 Wt. W14957/M90 750,000 1/16 J.B.C. & A. Forms/C.2118/12.

Instructions regarding War Diaries and Intelligence Summaries are contained in F. S. Regs., Part II. and the Staff Manual respectively. Title Pages will be prepared in manuscript.

WAR DIARY
or
INTELLIGENCE SUMMARY

(Erase heading not required.)

Army Form C. 2118.

Place	Date	Hour	Summary of Events and Information	Remarks and references to Appendices
U.14 C 1.2 COMBLES 1/10,000	25.12.16		Started upon wiring our line in front of No 4 Coy during the night – continued working on the communication trench & laid duckboarding down between support Coy. H.Q. and No 3 Coy. H.Q. as well as other work.	
			Our artillery shelled the back areas of the enemy lines at fixed periods during the day.	
			The Adjutant visited the front line at night.	
	26.12.16		General the Hon. W. Lambton. G.O.C. IV Div with Brig Gen J.B. Seeley & Col. Forster R. Warwickshire Regt (acting Brig Gen) came round the reserve line in the morning.	
			Hostile. Aeroplanes very active in the morning – later our aeroplanes entered upon the scene & some fighting took place. Four aeroplanes were seen to fall, but their nationality was not definitely known.	
			Work was continued during the night & a fair amount of improvement was achieved in spite of very adverse weather conditions, & extremely bad trenches to work upon.	
			Capt. Kirkwood visited the front line at night.	
			Capt. Pelly went back to rest for 24 hours, and Mr. Duke took over the command of No 3 Coy in the front line. During this time the front line had been relieved one platoon per Coy. at a time every twenty four hours to ensure the men getting that amount of rest, during the 4 days in COMBLES. Coy officers in the front line were also relieved	J.M. Kirkwood Capt

2449 Wt. W14957/M90 750,000 1/16 J.B.C. & A. Forms/C.2118/12.

Army Form C. 2118.

WAR DIARY
or
~~INTELLIGENCE SUMMARY~~

(Erase heading not required.)

Instructions regarding War Diaries and Intelligence Summaries are contained in F. S. Regs., Part II. and the Staff Manual respectively. Title Pages will be prepared in manuscript.

Place	Date	Hour	Summary of Events and Information	Remarks and references to Appendices
U.14.C.1.2 COMBLES 1/10,000	27.12.16		Brig. Gen. Gosling the new Brigadier Comdg 10th Bde visited our line in the morning. Work was continued as usual during the night. Enemies artillery fairly active in the neighbourhood of our support trenches but no casualties occurred. Major Sir George Lacon Bart. with the H.Q. Warwickshire Regt. arrived at our Battn. HQ at 4 pm. Our guides met their relief Coys at 4-30 pm at the FREGICOURT X Rds. The relief was not completed until 9-15 pm. One man was killed, & one wounded by snipers to-day. The Battn. marched back by Platoons to go into Bde reserve at Camp X near MAURE PAS HALTE. Owing to the enemy shelling the FREGICOURT-COMBLES Rd. with gas shells the return march was considerably hampered, whilst one platoon suffered three casualties having got into the gas zone without realizing the situation. About 12 midnight everyone was reported to be in Camp. Lt Col. W.R. Portal joined the Battn. on its arrival in Camp, having returned from hospital. Lieut Carrick and 60 other ranks joined the Battn. from the Reserve Regt.	
Camp X MAUREPAS HALTE	28.12.16		All men who had been through the gas zone last night were ordered to rest as much as possible during the day. Casualties for our four days in the trenches Officers nil O.R. killed 3 wounded (including gas) 6	J. [illegible]

2449 Wt. W14957/M90 750,000 1/16 J.B.C. & A. Forms/C.2118/12.

Instructions regarding War Diaries and Intelligence Summaries are contained in F. S. Regs., Part II. and the Staff Manual respectively. Title Pages will be prepared in manuscript.

WAR DIARY
or
INTELLIGENCE SUMMARY

(Erase heading not required.)

Army Form C. 2118.

Place	Date	Hour	Summary of Events and Information	Remarks and references to Appendices
Camp X MAUREPAS HALTE	29.12.16		Capt. Lord Stanley and Lieut. J.H. Robinson went to Hospital. Our total ~~number~~ of men reported as suffering from trench feet as the result of our last tour in the trenches amounts to 29 cases to date – every precaution had been taken previous to going up to the trenches i.e. foot rubbing every day & the daily use of whale oil whilst every man took up dry socks with him, & when relieved they returned to COMBLES – where their feet were rubbed, & their boots and socks changed.	
	30.12.16		The Battn. paraded at 2 pm ~~and~~ embussed at 2-30 pm and went into Corps reserve at Camp 112. [ALBERT 1/40,000. L 2.c 9.9.]	
CAMP. 112	31.12.16		Re-organizing & refitting. 1. N.C.O. & 5 men left to report to No I Salvage Section.	

[signature] Capt.

2449 Wt. W14957/M90 750,000 1/16 J.B.C. & A. Forms/C.2118/12.

4th Division

War Diaries

10th Infantry Bde

Household Battn.

January. To June

1917

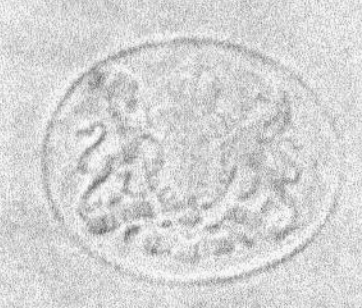

Vol 3

CONFIDENTIAL.

WAR DIARY

OF

HOUSEHOLD BATTALION.

From 1st. January, 1917. To 31st. January, 1917.

Instructions regarding War Diaries and Intelligence Summaries are contained in F. S. Regs., Part II. and the Staff Manual respectively. Title Pages will be prepared in manuscript.

WAR DIARY
or
INTELLIGENCE SUMMARY
(Erase heading not required.)

Army Form C. 2118.

Place	Date	Hour	Summary of Events and Information	Remarks and references to Appendices
CAMP.112	1.1.17		work under Coy arrangements	
			3 N.C.O's and 47 men left the Battn to be attached for duty ~~with~~ to the IV Div. Works Battn	
" "	2.1.17		2nd Lieuts L. Bonham-Carter and R. Boyd joined the Battn from the Reserve Battn	
			5. N.C.O's, 25 men & 1 Coy Cook left to be attached for duty to the IV Div. Works Battn	
			Work under Coy. arrangements, and cleaning up round the huts. 2/Lt H. C. NELSON struck off the strength	
	3.1.17		Lieut. Col W R PORTAL evacuated through 11th Field Ambulance.	
			C. of H. FOSTER and 30 O.R. sent to 4th DIV. Works Battn.	
			Parades for cleaning of camp and kit. Wash-house, officers cookhouse and latrine erected.	
	4.1.17		Parades for training. Lewis Gunners and Signallers to be trained.	
			Platoon training 8-30 - 10-30. Company training 10-30 - 12-30. Bayonet fighting 2 - 3.30 p.m.	
			Wet Canteen opened.	
			Lieut. OLIVER evacuated through 11th Field Ambulance.	
			2nd Lieut. B.N. GIBBS struck off the strength.	
			[signature] Lieut. & A/Adjt.	

2449 Wt. W14957/M90 750,000 1/16 J.B.C. & A. Forms/C.2118/12.

Army Form C. 2118.

Instructions regarding War Diaries and Intelligence Summaries are contained in F. S. Regs., Part II. and the Staff Manual respectively. Title Pages will be prepared in manuscript.

WAR DIARY
or
INTELLIGENCE SUMMARY
(Erase heading not required.)

Place	Date	Hour	Summary of Events and Information	Remarks and references to Appendices
CAMP 112	5.1.17.		Platoon and Company training.	
			Lieut. F.R. HAGGIE struck off the strength. dated 28.12.16.	
			C. of H. SELLERS to works Battn.	
	6.1.17		Platoon and Company training.	
	7.1.17		IV Div. holiday. Divine Service 11 a.m.	
			Christmas dinners 1 p.m.	
	8.1.17		Training.	
			Lieuts. DUKE and GODFREY granted leave to PARIS 8.1.17 – 10.1.17.	
	9.		Training. 2nd Lts. DAKEYNE and DAVIES evacuated through 11th Field Ambulance.	
			Lieut. BRIDGEMAN to Gas-course at IV Div. Anti-Gas School.	
			Football – LAMBTON CUP 1st ROUND. 2nd SEAFORTH HIGHLANDERS 6 – H.B. Nil.	
	10.		Training.	
	11		2nd Lts. Du TYRWHITT-DRAKE and W. GREEN joined Battn from Reserve Battn.	
	12		Training.	
	13		Lieut BRIDGEMAN returned from Gas course.	
	14.		Lieut. A.P. GODFREY to SNIPING course. Lts R.E. DUKE and TYRWHITT-DRAKE to IV Div. School OISEMONT.	[illegible signature] Lt. Col.

2449 Wt. W14957/M90 750,000 1/16 J.B.C. & A. Forms/C.2118/12.

Instructions regarding War Diaries and Intelligence Summaries are contained in F. S. Regs., Part II. and the Staff Manual respectively. Title Pages will be prepared in manuscript.

WAR DIARY
or
INTELLIGENCE SUMMARY
(Erase heading not required.)

Army Form C. 2118.

Place	Date	Hour	Summary of Events and Information	Remarks and references to Appendices
Camp 112	15.1.17		Clearing up camp preparatory to move.	
			2nd Lieut. W. GREEN to Bde. Bombing class.	
	16.		Moved from Camp 112 to Camp 18 (G 10 c) 1 mile E. of SUZANNE.	
			Reached new camp 3. p.m.	
			Fall of snow during night.	
	17		Parade 2.30 p.m. Met guides at MOULIN de FARGNY at 4.30 p.m. Marched via CURLU, Bois de HEM, BOYAU WARY, to right sub-sector of trenches C 21 c 1.7 to C 26 a 9.5. 10th Inf. Bde relieving part of 18th French Div. Household Battn relieved 32nd Regt. Commandant PEYRE. Relief delayed owing to No. 2 Coy guide misleading Coy and allowing two Coys. of WARWICKS to cut in ahead.	
			Relief reported complete 3.30 a.m. One man fell out only, after a very trying march with men heavily laden.	
			Trench strength 11 Officers 295 O.R. with 2 Officers, 123 O.R from WARWICKS.	
			Dispositions Right Sub. Sector (Lieut. PORTAL, Lt BRIDGEMAN, 2/Lt. BOYD.	
			L.P. No. 1 — 1 N.C.O and 4 men	
			" " 2. — 2 Lewis Guns and bombing post - 20 men in all Really a small redoubt.	
			" " 3 — 1 N.C.O and 3 men	

R. [illegible] Lt. a/adjt.

2449 Wt. W14957/M90 750,000 1/16 J.B.C. & A. Forms/C.2118/12.

Instructions regarding War Diaries and Intelligence Summaries are contained in F. S. Regs., Part II. and the Staff Manual respectively. Title Pages will be prepared in manuscript.

WAR DIARY
or
INTELLIGENCE SUMMARY
(Erase heading not required.)

Army Form C. 2118.

Place	Date	Hour	Summary of Events and Information	Remarks and references to Appendices
	17.		Disposition Right Sub-sector (continued) Coy. H.Q. and support line in BOURDIC Trench 29 men. D'Apremont trench being impassable was blocked and a bombing post established. Two Bde M.G's in this sector. Left Sub-sector. No. 2 Coy under Capt. TOBIN and 2/Lieut CARRICK. L.P. 4 1 N.C.O and 4 men. " " 5 not held as post is isolated and fire covered by M.G fire " " 6 1 N.C.O + 4 men. Between posts three platoons of 20 men each who find reliefs for L.P.s. Each with a L.G. Coy. H.Q and support line 22 men and 1 L.G. 2 Bde. M.G's in this sector. SUPPORT LINE. No. 4 Coy. 84 men under Capt BODINGTON. 2nd Lieut RECK, in dug-outs on left + right of BETHUNE - PERONNE road. "D" Coy. WARWICKS - 123 men under 2nd Lieut ILES on E of road. Battn. H.Q. at P.C. THERON on BETHUNE road opposite entrance to BOYAU WARY.	R. [illegible] Lt. a/Adjt

2449 Wt. W14957/M90 750,000 1/16 J.B.C. & A. Forms/C.2118/12.

Army Form C. 2118.

Instructions regarding War Diaries and Intelligence Summaries are contained in F. S. Regs., Part II. and the Staff Manual respectively. Title Pages will be prepared in manuscript.

WAR DIARY
or
INTELLIGENCE SUMMARY

(Erase heading not required.)

Place	Date	Hour	Summary of Events and Information	Remarks and references to Appendices
	17/18		Communication established from Battn. Hdqrs to left and right sub-sectors.	
			" " right subsector to 90th French Infantry – 150 yds away	
			" " left " to 2nd SEAFORTHS.	
			" " Battn Hdqrs to Support Battn (WARWICKS) at ROAD WOOD (BOIS MADAME) and Bde. Hdqrs at BOIS de HEM.	
			Condition of trenches much better than anything we have had yet. Communication by day to both sectors. Dug-outs for all men off duty. Front line impassable in several places. C of H. MARRIAGE with platoon and Lewis Gun isolated by day behind NO. 4 L.P. Duck-boards intermittent through all trenches.	
			NO. 3 Coy. Owing to shortage of No's 1 & 2 Coys. 2 platoons of No. 3 under 2nd Lieut WHITELAW with Capt. TOBIN in his support line, 2 platoons under C. of H REYNOLDS with Lieut PORTAL. Capt. MALCOLM. C.M. WRIGHT i/c of Battn Dump.	
			INTELLIGENCE From French reports enemy in front is 103RD SAXONS REGT. GERMAN wire good. Enemy quiet except for aerial torpedoes and intermittent shelling.	
			WORK owing to fatigue of men and lateness of relief little done except opening communication trench to Rt Coy and carrying water S.A.A. & grenades to front line.	R. P. Dill [?] Lt. Adjt.

2449 Wt. W14957/M90 750,000 1/16 J.B.C. & A. Forms/C.2118/12.

Army Form C. 2118.

Instructions regarding War Diaries and Intelligence Summaries are contained in F. S. Regs., Part II. and the Staff Manual respectively. Title Pages will be prepared in manuscript.

WAR DIARY
or
INTELLIGENCE SUMMARY
(Erase heading not required.)

Place	Date	Hour	Summary of Events and Information	Remarks and references to Appendices
C 21 c 1.7 C 26 a 9.5 Ref 1/10.000. Trench map. 57C NW4 BOUCHAVESNES	18.	3.55 A.M.	Relief reported complete to Bde. Hdqrs. No casualties. Capt KIRKWOOD reconnoitred the whole position by daylight. D'APREMONT trench thoroughly blocked and bombing post strengthened. 4 G.S. command good field of fire. Situation satisfactory. From left sub-sector visual communication with support line of SEAFORTHS. German listening post 20 yds in front of No 6 L.P. Situation satisfactory. Distance to Germans on whole front 150 - 200 yds. All L.Ps except No 2 isolated by day. WORK Battn dump established near Battn. Hdqrs. Much work done on improvement of trenches and clearing of mud, frost making work easier. BOYAU GALTRINEL (to left subsector) cleared out. Latrines perfected. Water, grenades, S.A.A carried to front line. Wire, pickets, trench boards indented for. ARTILLERY normal. Valley between BOIS MARRIERES and BOUCHAVESNES shelled intermittently. Trench mortar fire active into trench between our right Coy. and French. REINFORCEMENT of 18 O.R. reported at our 1st line transport at MOULIN de FARGNY.	[signature] Lt. [illegible]

2449 Wt. W14957/M90 750,000 1/16 J.B.C. & A. Forms/C.2118/12.

Army Form C. 2118.

Instructions regarding War Diaries and Intelligence Summaries are contained in F. S. Regs., Part II. and the Staff Manual respectively. Title Pages will be prepared in manuscript.

WAR DIARY
or
INTELLIGENCE SUMMARY
(Erase heading not required.)

Place	Date	Hour	Summary of Events and Information	Remarks and references to Appendices
	19.		Brigadier-General GOSLING and Capt. FELLOWES (Bde. Major) came round front line. Brigade had been anxious about our communication on right, but General was satisfied with dispositions. Operations. (a) During night 18/19 enemy's patrol driven off by L.G. fire from left sub-sector. (b) Intermittent sniping all day. (c) Trench between Rt. Coy and French badly knocked about by aerial torpedoes, whizz-bangs and rifle-grenades. INTELLIGENCE. 2/Lieut BOYD took patrol to French during the night. He reported that they had M.G. on their extreme left 75 yds from L.P. No. 1 covering blank space between us. WORK. Wire taken up to front line and our wire improved in many places. Parapets strengthened and improved. Front line trench to right of Rt. Coy found quite impassable and blocked. Trench boards taken up to front line. General improvement of whole system. ARTILLERY evenly distributed, not heavy on either side. Gas alert. German wireless intercepted "British relieving French on night of 19th/20th." All ranks warned and whole line on the alert. No hostile action by enemy. REINFORCEMENT of 18 OR. sent to front line. 9 Men sent to 178th Tunnelling Coy. 4 " " " WORKS BATTN.	R. J. ... Lieut. & Adjt.

2449 Wt. W14957/M90 750,000 1/16 J.B.C. & A. Forms/C.2118/12.

Instructions regarding War Diaries and Intelligence Summaries are contained in F. S. Regs., Part II. and the Staff Manual respectively. Title Pages will be prepared in manuscript.

WAR DIARY
or
INTELLIGENCE SUMMARY
(Erase heading not required.)

Army Form C. 2118.

Place	Date	Hour	Summary of Events and Information	Remarks and references to Appendices
	20.		Major General Hon W. LAMBTON and Brig. General GOSLING inspected position from right-Subsector. General LAMBTON satisfied with dispositions which he said were much better than he had hoped.	
		11.25 a.m.	Message from Bde cancelling relief of front line for night of 20/21st and postponing it till 21st/22nd. This owing to reliefs occurring both on our right and left.	
			OPERATIONS (a) Our snipers active. Results uncertain. (b) Enemy M.G. fire intermittent through night. Snipers active all day. Trench mortar batteries quiet.	
			INTELLIGENCE Enemy trench mortar battery reported in front of P2 in enemy FONTENOY trench. C.O. inspected P1 and found position more satisfactory than he had anticipated. M.G. at junction of COMMERCY and communication trench leading to P1 in conjunction with our L.G. cross-fire covers whole front. Enemy aeroplane made reconnaissance over whole front 2-3.30 pm. M.G's opened fire, but without effect.	
			WORK DONE. Wiring front line. General improvement.	
			Rations brought up to Bde. Dump on pack ponies & carried to front line.	
			Casualties Wounded – 3 men from "D" Coy WARWICKS. All slight shrapnel wounds.	R. P. [illegible] Lt. adjt.

Instructions regarding War Diaries and Intelligence Summaries are contained in F. S. Regs., Part II. and the Staff Manual respectively. Title Pages will be prepared in manuscript.

WAR DIARY
or
INTELLIGENCE SUMMARY
(Erase heading not required.)

Army Form C. 2118.

Place	Date	Hour	Summary of Events and Information	Remarks and references to Appendices
	20		Artillery. Fairly active near left communication trench, Battn. Hdqrs and valley beyond. No harm done.	
	21		Operations (a) Trench mortars active on right sub-sector 11 p.m.-1 a.m. (20th/21st). Occasional bursts of M.G. fire. Snipers active.	
			(b) Our snipers trying to locate enemy's sniping posts.	
			INTELLIGENCE	
			Left Coy reported enemy's wire thin in front of them.	
			Enemy transport on BETHUNE Rd 500 yds. in front of L.P. No. 2. Matter reported. Road shelled later on.	
			Enemy M.G. located at junction FONTENOY - CALYPSO trenches.	
			Enemy aeroplane activity.	
			RELIEF. Right sector by 1st R. WARWICKS	
			Left " " 1st R. IRISH FUS.	
			Relieving Coys began to come in 6 p.m. in following order of relief.	
			C Coy relieve No. 1 in right sub-sector	
			A " " " 2 " left "	
			B " " " 4 & D Coy of WARWICKS in support.	
			Relief reported complete 8.15 p.m. without casualty.	
			Battn. proceeded after relief to Bde. Reserve at Bois de HEM	
			1FC	R. M. Dill? Lt. & Adjt.

2449 Wt. W14957/M90 750,000 1/16 J.B.C. & A. Forms/C.2118/12.

Instructions regarding War Diaries and Intelligence Summaries are contained in F. S. Regs., Part II. and the Staff Manual respectively. Title Pages will be prepared in manuscript.

Army Form C. 2118.

WAR DIARY
or
INTELLIGENCE SUMMARY

(Erase heading not required.)

Place	Date	Hour	Summary of Events and Information	Remarks and references to Appendices
	21		P.C. CURRAGES by valley track near RAILWAY and BOYAU des GLANDS. Got in at 11.15 p.m. only one man falling out on the way. Hot tea for men on arrival.	
			CASUALTIES during day	
			Wounded 3196/2LG. Tpr PART No. 3 Coy Shell wound thigh.	
			3825/13874 " PARTRIDGE " " " " arm.	
			3557/13 1109 " COOPER " 4 "	
	22		25 men sent with gas-gongs to app. sub-sector (1st R. Irish Fus.)	
			100 " under 2nd Lt. RICE sent to work on communication trench with SEAFORTHS at ROAD WOOD.	
			2nd Lieut. F.R. DAKEYNE reported from Hospital.	
			Day spent in cleaning.	
			Men in long dug-outs with bunks.	
	23		Aeroplane activity. Air fight. German machine seen to fall in flames towards BOUCHAVESNES. another enemy machine brought down.	
			Relief Battn. relieved from Bde Reserve by 20th R. Fusiliers 98th Bde. 33rd Div.	
			Relief complete 6.30 p.m.	
			Battn marched to SUZANNE. Accomodated in billets. 10th Bde. Hdqrs in CHATEAU.	[illegible signature]

2449 Wt. W14957/M90 750,000 1/16 J.B.C. & A. Forms/C.2118/12.

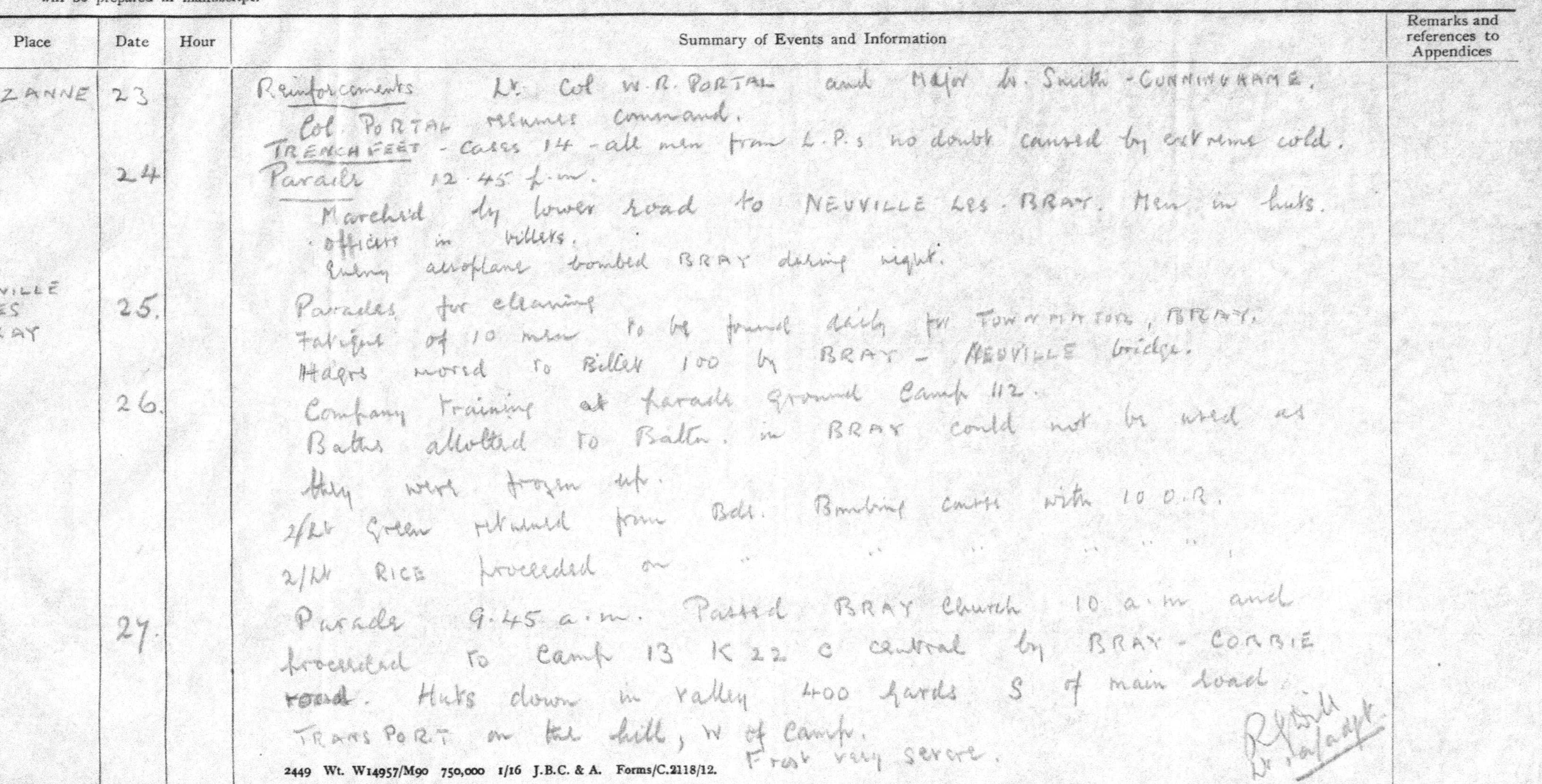

Instructions regarding War Diaries and Intelligence Summaries are contained in F. S. Regs., Part II. and the Staff Manual respectively. Title Pages will be prepared in manuscript.

WAR DIARY
or
INTELLIGENCE SUMMARY
(Erase heading not required.)

Army Form C. 2118.

Place	Date	Hour	Summary of Events and Information	Remarks and references to Appendices
SUZANNE	23		Reinforcements Lt. Col W. R. PORTAL and Major [illegible] Smith-CUNNINGHAME. Col. PORTAL resumes command. TRENCH FEET - cases 14 - all men from L. P. s no doubt caused by extreme cold.	
	24		Parade 12.45 p.m. Marched by lower road to NEUVILLE LES-BRAY. Men in huts. officers in billets. Enemy aeroplane bombed BRAY during night.	
NEUVILLE LES BRAY	25.		Parades for cleaning. Fatigue of 10 men to be found daily for TOWN MAJOR, BRAY. Hdqrs moved to Billet 100 by BRAY - NEUVILLE bridge.	
	26.		Company training at parade ground Camp 112. Baths allotted to Battn. in BRAY could not be used as they were frozen up. 2/Lt Green returned from Bde. Bombing course with 10 O.R. 2/Lt RICE proceeded on " " "	
	27.		Parade 9.45 a.m. Passed BRAY Church 10 a.m. and proceeded to Camp 13 K 22 c central by BRAY - CORBIE ~~road~~. Huts down in valley 400 yards S of main road. TRANSPORT on the hill, W of Camp. Frost very severe.	

R. J. [illegible]
Lt. & Adjt.

2449 Wt. W14957/M90 750,000 1/16 J.B.C. & A. Forms/C.2118/12.

Instructions regarding War Diaries and Intelligence Summaries are contained in F. S. Regs., Part II. and the Staff Manual respectively. Title Pages will be prepared in manuscript.

WAR DIARY
or
INTELLIGENCE SUMMARY
(Erase heading not required.)

Army Form C. 2118.

Place	Date	Hour	Summary of Events and Information	Remarks and references to Appendices
CAMP 13 K22c central. 1/40.000 ALBERT.	28.		Company training. Training of raiding parties under 2/Lts CARRICK (No. 2 Coy) and 2nd Lt. WHITELAW (No. 3 Coy). Parties composed of 24 men including L G team, bombers and wirers. Programme of training 8.30 to 10.30 Coy training / Raiding parties. — Lewis gun classes under Cpls. BUCKINGHAM + SADDLER. 11.15 - 12.30 Battn. Parade for DRILL 2. - 3.30. Coy training / Raiding parties. — Lewis gun class. Bombing N.C.O.s class.	
	29		Parades for training as in yesterday's programme.	
	30.		Training. Accident. At 11.30 a.m. an accident took place from an explosion in the incinerator. Pte SIZER (No. 1 Coy) Pte EMERY (No 3 Coy) while doing sanitary duties near incinerator were wounded. Pte SIZER - arm & head Pte EMERY arm and leg. Cause of explosion unexplained	R. J. Dill [?] Lt. Adjt.

2449 Wt. W14957/M90 750,000 1/16 J.B.C. & A. Forms/C.2118/12.

Instructions regarding War Diaries and Intelligence Summaries are contained in F. S. Regs., Part II. and the Staff Manual respectively. Title Pages will be prepared in manuscript.

WAR DIARY
or
INTELLIGENCE SUMMARY
(Erase heading not required.)

Army Form C. 2118.

Place	Date	Hour	Summary of Events and Information	Remarks and references to Appendices
CAMP 13	31		Training for Coys. as per programme.	
			Court of inquiry into accident to Ptr. SIBER and Ptr. EMERY.	
			Bdr. General GOSLING inspected CAMP 13 in afternoon.	
			Lieut. T H ROBINSON evacuated sick to ENGLAND dated 21.1.17.	

R [illegible] Lt. Col. [illegible]

2449 Wt. W14957/M90 750,000 1/16 J.B.C. & A. Forms/C.2118/12.

Vol 4

- CONFIDENTIAL -

WAR DIARY

OF

HOUSEHOLD BATTALION.

FROM:- 4TH. FEBRUARY. 1917. TO:- 3RD MARCH, 1917.

Instructions regarding War Diaries and Intelligence Summaries are contained in F. S. Regs., Part II. and the Staff Manual respectively. Title Pages will be prepared in manuscript.

WAR DIARY
or
INTELLIGENCE SUMMARY
(Erase heading not required.)

Army Form C. 2118.

Place	Date	Hour	Summary of Events and Information	Remarks and references to Appendices
CAMP 13.	1.2.17		Company training. Raiding parties bombing. Capt. MALCOLM, Lt PORTAL, 2/Lt SANDFORD admitted to Hospital. Warning order received to move to BRAY.	
	2.2.17		Cleaned camp preparatory to move.	
			Major KIRKWOOD proceeded on 10 days leave to ENGLAND.	
			Capt BODINGTON admitted to hospital.	
BRAY SUR SOMME.			Parade 1 p.m. Marched to BRAY by CORBIE road. Took up billets in the town. No. 1 Coy. RUE de CORBIE. No 2 Coy CAFÉ de la PLACE. No's 3 & 4 in TOWN HALL. Battn Hdqrs. 4 RUE de GAMBETTA.	
	3.2.17		Coy. training on parade ground at CAMP 112.	
			30 men for TOWN MAJOR'S fatigue.	
	4.2.17		Sunday	
			Divine Service 11 a.m in Town Hall. All men attended.	
			R.C. 10 a.m in BRAY CHURCH.	
			Presbyterian 2.30 p.m in Town Hall.	
			2nd Lieut W. R. CARRICK and 10 O.R. proceeded on Bde. Bombing class at CAMP 112.	
			2nd Lieut. RICE and 10. O.R returned from Bde. Bombing course. 2nd Lieut. RICE and 8 O.R. as qualified bombers. 1 man sustained injury to left ear from shrapnel and therefore could not throw.	

2449 Wt. W14957/M90 750,000 1/16 J.B.C. & A. Forms/C.2118/12.

Army Form C. 2118.

Instructions regarding War Diaries and Intelligence Summaries are contained in F. S. Regs., Part II. and the Staff Manual respectively. Title Pages will be prepared in manuscript.

WAR DIARY
or
INTELLIGENCE SUMMARY
(Erase heading not required.)

Place	Date	Hour	Summary of Events and Information	Remarks and references to Appendices
BRAY SUR SOMME	4.II.17		News from XVth Corps that AMERICA has broken off diplomatic relations with Germany and called on all other neutral countries to do the same.	
	5.II.17		Major SMITH-CUNNINGHAME, Capt. TOBIN, 2nd Lieuts DAKEYNE and RICE and 160 O.R. proceeded to P.C. BONNET (B 21 c. 2.8. ref 1/20000 62 c N.W.) for work on mined dug-outs under 178th Tunnelling Coy. To be accommodated there. Advance under 2/Lieut RICE left at 8 a.m. Remainder at 10.30 a.m. Party composed as follows:— No 1 Coy 36 O.R. " 2 " 42 " " 3 " 8 " " 4 " 74 " (including C.Q.S. HANCOCK, cooks and cookers).	
	6.II.		Fatigue found for digging at Bde. Grenade School. No. 396 Pte PEPPER to England for commission. Lewis Gun classes continued.	
	7-8th		Fatigues. Preparation to move up to the line	R.J. Worth [illegible]

2449 Wt. W14957/M90 750,000 1/16 J.B.C. & A. Forms/C.2118/12.

Instructions regarding War Diaries and Intelligence Summaries are contained in F. S. Regs., Part II. and the Staff Manual respectively. Title Pages will be prepared in manuscript.

WAR DIARY
or
INTELLIGENCE SUMMARY
(Erase heading not required.)

Army Form C. 2118.

Place	Date	Hour	Summary of Events and Information	Remarks and references to Appendices
BRAY – CAMP 17 N. of SUZANNE	9th		Parade – 9.0 a.m. No. 3 Coy & details of Nos 1. 2 & 4 under Lieut. GODFREY marched to camp 17, N. of SUZANNE.	
			2/Lt C. J. PYM rejoined from hospital.	
			2/Lt. E. H. DAVIES struck off strength – 28/1/17 having been evacuated to England.	
	10th		Parade 1 p.m.	
ASQUITH FLATS B16 d 8.2.			Relieved 1st WORCESTERSHIRE Regt in Bde. Reserve at ASQUITH FLATS (B 16 d 8.2.) Marched by MARICOURT – RED FARM – PINNEYS POST. Relief complete at 4.30 p.m. 2/Lt CARRICK & 9 O.R. rejoined from Bde. Grenade School.	
	11th		MAJOR CUNNINGHAME and 160 O.R. rejoined from digging party at P.C. BONNET. Work has been digging gun emplacements close to RANCOURT.	
			Carrying party of 100 found 6 p.m. from CRANIERE dump to ANDOVER.	
	12th		CAPT. H.A. PELLY & C. of E. TWIDLE rejoined from IV ARMY SCHOOL	
			CAPT. J. McCUTCHEON R.A.M.C. transferred to 11th Field Ambulance.	[signature]

2449 Wt. W14957/M90 750,000 1/16 J.B.C. & A. Forms/C.2118/12.

Army Form C. 2118.

Instructions regarding War Diaries and Intelligence Summaries are contained in F. S. Regs., Part II. and the Staff Manual respectively. Title Pages will be prepared in manuscript.

WAR DIARY
or
INTELLIGENCE SUMMARY
(Erase heading not required.)

Place	Date	Hour	Summary of Events and Information	Remarks and references to Appendices
ASQUITH FLATS.	12th		Capt. J. F. M. SLOAN R.A.M.C. joined from 11th Field Ambulance.	
			Major-General W. LAMBTON inspected lines.	
			Heavy bombardment begun by our guns on German lines - continued from 5.30 a.m. to 5 p.m. 9.2's in CRAMIERS valley active all day.	
			C.O. went up to ALDERSHOT (C 8 d 4 8) - Battn. H.Qrs. of 1st WARWICKSHIRE Regt. Right Battn. in the line - to reconnoitre position. Very quiet so far & good conditions owing to frost. Few casualties.	
			225 men found for carrying parties.	
	13th		Outbreak of German measles in 2nd SEAFORTHS. They were relieved during day by 1st Battn. RIFLE BRIGADE (11th Bde) & proceeded to isolation camp - Camp 18 (E of SUZANNE).	
			CAPT. H. C. PEMBER reported from Base & was posted to No. 2 Coy.	
			2nd Lt. V. BOLITHO " " " " " 4 "	
			223 men found as carrying parties at night for R.E.	
	14th		Lt. O. S. PORTAL returned from hospital.	
			2/Lts. PYM & RICE, Cpls. HOBBS (No. 1) & FOLLETT (No. 4) to IVth Div. School. C. of R. SCRAGG to Musketry course, CAMBIERS.	

2449 Wt. W14957/M90 750,000 1/16 J.B.C. & A. Forms/C.2118/12.

[illegible signature]

Army Form C. 2118.

Instructions regarding War Diaries and Intelligence Summaries are contained in F. S. Regs., Part II. and the Staff Manual respectively. Title Pages will be prepared in manuscript.

WAR DIARY
or
INTELLIGENCE SUMMARY
(Erase heading not required.)

Place	Date	Hour	Summary of Events and Information	Remarks and references to Appendices
ASQUITH FLATS.	14th 2.17.	11 P.M.	General GOSLING + MAJOR KIRKWOOD returned from leave from England.	
			Carrying parties of 215 found at night.	
	15.2.17.		Battn furnished carrying party as before for front line.	
ALDERSHOT map ref. C8d 3.05.7 BOUCHAVESNES 1/10,000	16.2.17.		Battn relieved Royal Warwickshire Regt in front line trenches in area C9a96 (Map ref: BOUCHAVESNES 1/10.000.) Our line extended from point C9b83 to point C6b57 on the Right. The East Lancashire Regt. (12th Bde.) (temporarily attached to 10th Bde) were on our right + 1st Battn. RIFLE BRIGADE on our left. Our dispositions were as follows :-	
			Front line Right sub. sector	
			4 posts with a total of 4 NCO's and 25 men	
			3 Lewis Gun teams complete total 18 NCO's + men	
			= 47 NCO's + men	
			Left sub sector	
			4 posts with a total of 4 NCO'S and 22 men	
			2 Lewis Gun teams total 12 NCO'S + men	
			= 38 NCO's + men	Whitton Kirkwood Major

2449 Wt. W14957/M90 750,000 1/16 J.B.C. & A. Forms/C.2118/12.

Army Form C. 2118.

Instructions regarding War Diaries and Intelligence Summaries are contained in F. S. Regs., Part II. and the Staff Manual respectively. Title Pages will be prepared in manuscript.

WAR DIARY
or
INTELLIGENCE SUMMARY
(Erase heading not required.)

Place	Date	Hour	Summary of Events and Information	Remarks and references to Appendices
ALDERSHOT	16.2.17	(Contd)	SUPPORT LINE. Right Sub Sector 1 Lewis gun team and 7 men under Lieut Whitelaw at AQUARIUM (C.14.5.1) There was also a signal station at this point. Battn HQs were at ALDERSHOT. where there were two Lewis guns & gun teams. RESERVE were at ANDOVER. (C.9. a 8.3) under Major Cunninghame No. 2 Coy under Captain Tobin held the Left Sub-sector of the front line " 3 " " " Pelly " " right " " " " " Nos 1 & 4 Coys were in reserve. The total trench strength of the Battn after putting all available men, including band, servants etc was only 276 exclusive of Officers. The ~~weather~~ frost, which had been a very hard one, broke on the afternoon of the relief, consequently the trenches began to get slushy and wet. The relief went off without any hitch, but was very slow owing to the distance which we had to come up along the communication trenches, it was completed soon after midnight. There was a certain amount of enemy shelling during the night. J Hunter Kirkwood Major	

2449 Wt. W14957/M90 750,000 1/16 J.B.C. & A. Forms/C.2118/12.

Instructions regarding War Diaries and Intelligence Summaries are contained in F. S. Regs., Part II. and the Staff Manual respectively. Title Pages will be prepared in manuscript.

Army Form C. 2118.

WAR DIARY
or
INTELLIGENCE SUMMARY
(Erase heading not required.)

Place	Date	Hour	Summary of Events and Information	Remarks and references to Appendices
ALDERSHOT	17.2.17		The ~~[illegible]~~ reserve Coys from ANDOVER as well as part of the Royal Warwickshire Regt. furnished the carrying & working parties, but the men were so done up on arrival at the front line trenches that very little work was completed.	
			Nothing particular to report during the day. ~~Lieut~~ Colonel Portal and Major Kirkwood visited the front line trenches during the day as the weather was dull & foggy.	
			Working parties up as usual during the night, but the conditions were ~~[illegible]~~ worse than the previous night as the thaw set in very suddenly. Lieut Duke returned from the Div school, & left to do duty at the Base at Havre	
	18.2.17		Our front sectors were heavily bombarded by 4.2 ~~[illegible]~~ 5.9 Hows as well as by Trench-mortars from 5.20 Am and 6.10 Am and we had 2 men killed and 8 wounded. Our artillery responded with a counter-barrage which caused the enemy to stop their bombardment.	
			Weather was mild and there was a fog over the country so that the front line could be visited during daylight. Trenches very heavy and the carrying parties went along the top.	
	19.2.17		A certain amount of shelling took place but no harm done. Our Right Sub-sector reconnoitred in front of their line but there was nothing to report. Work was much impeded by the bad condition of the trenches. Weather still mild and foggy	
	~~[illegible]~~		No. 1 Coy relieved No 3 Company No. 4 " " " 2 " Captain Tobin remained in Command of the left Sub-Sector and Major Cunninghame relieved Captain Pelly.	

J Milton Kirkwood
Major

2449 Wt. W14957/M90 750,000 1/16 J.B.C. & A. Forms/C.2118/12.

Army Form C. 2118.

Instructions regarding War Diaries and Intelligence Summaries are contained in F. S. Regs., Part II. and the Staff Manual respectively. Title Pages will be prepared in manuscript.

WAR DIARY
or
INTELLIGENCE SUMMARY
(Erase heading not required.)

Place	Date	Hour	Summary of Events and Information	Remarks and references to Appendices
ALDERSHOT	20.2.17		Intermittent trench mortar bombardment, and some artillery action against our front line - Little harm done, however.	
			Lieut Colonel Jack, West Yorkshire Regt. came to settle the relief for the next day, as the 23rd Bde took over our line. The 12th Bde had already been relieved by the 8th Div	
			Major General Lambton having gone on leave, Brig Gen Gosling took over the Division & Lieut Col Webber, Royal Irish Fusiliers went to the Bde.	
	21.2.17		Quiet day. weather mild & foggy.	
			Very little work was done in the front line system owing to the impossible condition of the trenches.	
			The relief which started early from ~~Anderson~~ ASQUITH FLATS was much impeded by heavy going, and congestion in the trenches. There was some delay after this in our left sub-sector owing to one of the relieving Lewis gun teams being exhausted.	
			In spite of this our relief was completed about 12-15 Am.	
			Headquarters went off as soon as the relief was reported complete - leaving the front line Coys to follow on, soup having been prepared for them at ALDERSHOT en route.	
			[signature] Major	

2449 Wt. W14957/M90 750,000 1/16 J.B.C. & A. Forms/C.2118/12.

Army Form C. 2118.

Instructions regarding War Diaries and Intelligence Summaries are contained in F. S. Regs., Part II. and the Staff Manual respectively. Title Pages will be prepared in manuscript.

WAR DIARY
or
INTELLIGENCE SUMMARY
(Erase heading not required.)

Place	Date	Hour	Summary of Events and Information	Remarks and references to Appendices
ALDERSHOT.	21.2.17	(Contd)	The following Casualties occurred during our turn in the trenches:–	
			Killed No 734 Spr. Dickson. 18.2.17	
			" 1707 " Anderson " " "	
			" 1896 " Woodhouse " " "	
			" 709 Cpl. Morris 19.2.17	
			Missing, believed killed	
			No. 404. Spr. Derx. 19.2.17	
			Died of Wounds	
			No. 836. Spr. Birket 24.2.17	
			" 888 " Thompson 18.2.17	
			Wounded 360 Cpl. Wood. 18.2.17	
			457 Spr. King " " "	
			481 " Needle " " "	
			" Brady " " "	
			accidentally wounded 469. Spr. Marshall 18.2.17	
			1139 " Slee 21.2.17	

[signature] Major

2449 Wt. W14957/M90 750,000 1/16 J.B.C. & A. Forms/C.2118/12.

Instructions regarding War Diaries and Intelligence Summaries are contained in F. S. Regs., Part II. and the Staff Manual respectively. Title Pages will be prepared in manuscript.

WAR DIARY
or
INTELLIGENCE SUMMARY
(Erase heading not required.)

Army Form C. 2118.

Place	Date	Hour	Summary of Events and Information	Remarks and references to Appendices
Camp 13 K 22. C Central ALBERT 1/40000.	22.2.17		The march back was a very tiring one for the men owing to the mud & bad state of the Trench boards. Lorries were waiting for the battalion at CRUCIFIX CORNER, MAUREPAS. The two Co's from the front line did not arrive at Camp 13 until 10 AM. They were very tired & footsore. Eighteen men were unaccounted for.	
	23.2.17.		All the absentees were accounted for by the evening. The men who had been working with the Road Batt: under Lieut Bower rejoined. Men spent the day cleaning up.	
	24.2.17		Cleaning kit & equipment	
	25.2.17		Church ~~Parades~~ Services were held in the huts	
	26.2.17.		Company Training began. Special attention being paid to platoon & section organization. Specialist classes for Lewis Gunners, bombers, signallers & wiring under specialist officers.	
	27.2.17.		Most of the Batt: being on fatigue specialist classes only were held	
	28.2.17		Company Training.	
	1.3.17		" "	
	~~2.3~~			
	2.3.17		Route march & specialist classes	
	3.3.17		Company training & specialist classes	

John [illegible] Major
Comdg [illegible] Batt.

2449 Wt. W14957/M90 750,000 1/16 J.B.C. & A. Forms/C.2118/12.

Instructions regarding War Diaries and Intelligence Summaries are contained in F. S. Regs., Part II. and the Staff Manual respectively. Title Pages will be prepared in manuscript.

WAR DIARY
or
INTELLIGENCE SUMMARY
(Erase heading not required.)

Army Form C. 2118.

Vol 5

Place	Date	Hour	Summary of Events and Information	Remarks and references to Appendices
CAMP 13 K22 c central. (ALBERT 1/40.000)	1.3.17		Coy training.	
	2 "		" "	
			Lt BRIDGEMAN 1 O.R. proceeded on Lewis Gun course, ETAPLES.	
	3 "		Coy: training	
CORBIE.	4 "		Battn marched to CORBIE en route for IIIrd ARMY area.	
			Battn left CAMP 13 at 11.15 a.m. arrived CORBIE 2.30 p.m.	
			Men in billets. Draft of 126 O.R. from 1st LANCS FUSILIERS, 2nd E. LANCS, KINGS OWN (Liverpool Regt), 21st W. YORKS.	
			Detacht. of 2nd SEAFORTHS accompanied Battn under Capt. DAVIDSON - Capt MACKAY assuming command at CORBIE.	
			MAJOR W. SMITH-CUNNINGHAME left Battn to join 10th CAMERONIANS - 46th DIV: as 2nd in command.	
	5 "		Battn moved from CORBIE to billets at BERTANGLES.	
BERTANGLES. D/1 Map AMIENS Sh 17, 1/100.000			Left CORBIE at 11 a.m. arrived BERTANGLES 5 p.m. March much delayed by transport as far as QUERRIEU. At IV ARMY H.Q. at QUERRIEU Battn. was inspected marching past by General Sir Henry RAWLINSON, commanding IV Army.	

R. F. Walker [?] Lt Col

2449 Wt. W14957/M90 750,000 1/16 J.B.C. & A. Forms/C.2118/12.

Army Form C. 2118.

Instructions regarding War Diaries and Intelligence Summaries are contained in F. S. Regs., Part II. and the Staff Manual respectively. Title Pages will be prepared in manuscript.

WAR DIARY
or
INTELLIGENCE SUMMARY
(Erase heading not required.)

Place	Date	Hour	Summary of Events and Information	Remarks and references to Appendices
BEAUVAL D/5 ref LENS 1/100 000.	6.3.17		Battn. left BERTANGLES 10.15 a.m arriving at BEAUVAL at 2.15 p.m. Billets were not quite ready – all in billets by 3.30 p.m.	
VILLERS-L'HOPITAL C/4 LENS 1/100.000	7.3.17		Battn. left BEAUVAL at 9.37 a.m & marched viâ DOULENS & FROHEN-le-GRAND to VILLERS-L'HOPITAL arriving 2.45 p.m. Billets inferior to any on the march so far. Warned that we are to stay for a fortnight for strenuous training.	
"	8.3.17		Day of rest in billets. Men very tired after long days of marching.	
"	9.3.17		Strenuous training started, by platoons. O. C. Coys. No. 1 Lieut. Godfrey. No. 2 Capt Tobin. No. 3 Capt Pelly. No. 4 Capt. Bodington.	
"	10.3.17		Platoon & Coy. training, continued. Two lines of trenches dug. Bombing & Lewis Gun classes.	

R. J. Wilk[illegible]

2449 Wt. W14957/M90 750,000 1/16 J.B.C. & A. Forms/C.2118/12.

Army Form C. 2118.

WAR DIARY
or
INTELLIGENCE SUMMARY
(Erase heading not required.)

Instructions regarding War Diaries and Intelligence Summaries are contained in F. S. Regs., Part II. and the Staff Manual respectively. Title Pages will be prepared in manuscript.

Place	Date	Hour	Summary of Events and Information	Remarks and references to Appendices
VILLERS - L'HOPITAL	11.3.17		Warning order to move.	
PETIT-BOURET SUR CANCHE G 33 SH 51 C 1/40.000	12.3.17		Battalion marched from VILLERS - L'HOPITAL to PETIT-BOURET - 1½ Kms beyond FREVENT. Parade 9 a.m. In to billets by 2 p.m.	
			Reinforcement of 3 officers and 164 O.R arrived at 4.15 p.m. Capt. Tenlon, 2/Lts BUCHANAN & LOWRIE	
			Reinforcement divided into Coys. - No 1. 52 No 2. 52 No 3 30. No 4. 30 & divided again into platoons.	

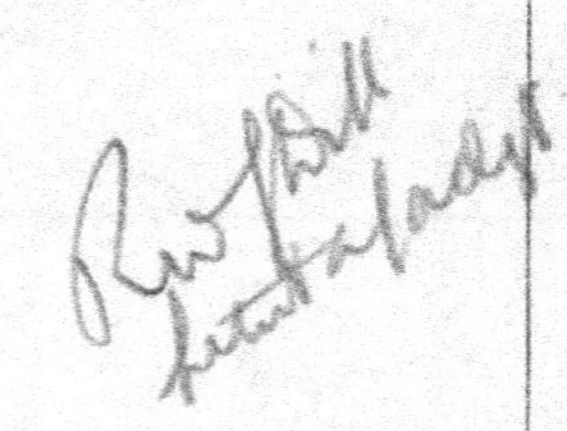

Instructions regarding War Diaries and Intelligence Summaries are contained in F. S. Regs., Part II. and the Staff Manual respectively. Title Pages will be prepared in manuscript.

Army Form C. 2118.

WAR DIARY
or
INTELLIGENCE SUMMARY
(Erase heading not required.)

Place	Date	Hour	Summary of Events and Information	Remarks and references to Appendices
PETIT BOURET SUR CANCHE MR G. 38. central FRANCE. Sheet 51c 1/40,000		13.3.17	Left PETIT BOURET at 9 Am and marched via BERLENCOURT and AMBRINES to SAVY where the Battn were billeted in tents. Re-inforcement men felt the march very much	
SAVY D. 4. d. 7. 6		14.3.17	Left SAVY at 9 Am and marched to LARESSET and MAROEUIL. Nos 1, 2 & 3 Coys, transport and HQs went to LARESSET, and No 4 Coy to MAROEUIL for the purpose of working on the Artillery Amn dumps at these places. Marquees, Store & bell tents were taken on lorries. Map references were given for site of camps, & orders to pitch tents accordingly. On arrival the site at LARESSET was found to be very bad, it was also ascertained that fewer men were required at LARESSET and more at MAROEUIL. The Staff had not been conspicuous in assisting our arrangements. Camps were pitched, however, in accordance with the orders of the day.	
LARESSET K. 5. c. 8. 5		15.3.17	Battn HQ and Nos 2 & 3 Coys moved to MAROEUIL with camp equipment. Transport & No. 1 Coy under Lieut Godfrey remained at LARESSET. The work of unloading amn trains and stacking amn commenced	
		16.3.17	Transport moved to MAROEUIL. Work as usual.	
MAROEUIL F 27. c. 3. 5		17.3.17	Work as ~~usual~~ usual, excepting No 3 Coy who did platoon training	[illegible] Major Household Battn

2449 Wt. W14957/M90 750,000 1/16 J.B.C. & A. Forms/C.2118/12.

Instructions regarding War Diaries and Intelligence Summaries are contained in F. S. Regs., Part II. and the Staff Manual respectively. Title Pages will be prepared in manuscript.

WAR DIARY
or
INTELLIGENCE SUMMARY
(Erase heading not required.)

Army Form C. 2118.

Place	Date	Hour	Summary of Events and Information	Remarks and references to Appendices
MAROEUIL F27.c.35	18.3.17 19 .. 20 .. 21 .. 22 ..		Work of unloading and moving ammunition was continued. Working parties were busy at night as well as by day. The weather was very cold owing to strong northerly winds & snow and there was a certain amount of sickness in consequence, especially as the men had no tent boards. Ration strength averaged 575 all ranks.	
	23.3.17		The Battn moved to SAVY and camped in the same tents as it occupied on the 13/14 inst. The Devon Labour Battn relieved the 3 Coys at MAROEUIL, whilst No I Coy at LARESSET was relieved by a Durham Labour Battn.	
SAVY.	24.3.17		The Battn paraded at 9 Am and marched NW via BETHONSART and OURTON to CAMBLAIN-CHATELAIN where it went into billets – the best that had been seen since leaving the back area to go up to the SOMME. On arrival there a draft of three officers – Captn Malcolm and 2nd Lieuts H.G. Barker and S.F. Stockwood – and 184 other ranks joined the Battn from No I I.B.D. HAVRE.	Capt Malcolm had been in hospital.
CAMBLAIN-CHÂTELAIN I9 T19 1/40,000	25.3.17		Divine service in the morning. The rest of the day was spent in cleaning up and settling into billets. A training ground was selected – although the space was limited – and a scheme of training drawn up.	

[illegible]
Major

2449 Wt. W14957/M90 750,000 1/16 J.B.C. & A. Forms/C.2118/12.

Army Form C. 2118.

Instructions regarding War Diaries and Intelligence Summaries are contained in F. S. Regs., Part II. and the Staff Manual respectively. Title Pages will be prepared in manuscript.

WAR DIARY
or
INTELLIGENCE SUMMARY

(Erase heading not required.)

Place	Date	Hour	Summary of Events and Information	Remarks and references to Appendices
CAMBLAIN-CHÂTELAIN I 9 T 19 1/40000	26.3.17		Coy training, and specialist classes	
	27.3.17		ditto ditto	
	28.3.17		Route march. Lt Col. Pollok, Major Kirkwood, Capts Boddington & Petty & Lieut Godfrey went over to reconnoitre the tracks leading up to the front line trenches N.E. of ARRAS in accordance with Bde instructions. They returned the same evening.	
	29.3.17		Coy training & specialist classes much interrupted owing to the weather	
	30.3.17		ditto ditto ditto	
	31.3.17		Battn practiced the attack.	
			Reinforcement of 3 O.R arrived 1 a.m.	
			" 17 " " 3 p.m.	

… Kirkwood, Major

2449 Wt. W14957/M90 750,000 1/16 J.B.C. & A. Forms/C.2118/12.

10/4

Confidential

War Diary

of

Household Battalion

from

1st April 1917

to

30th April 1917.

Volume 6.

[illegible]

Lieut Colonel

Commanding

Household Battalion

Vol 6

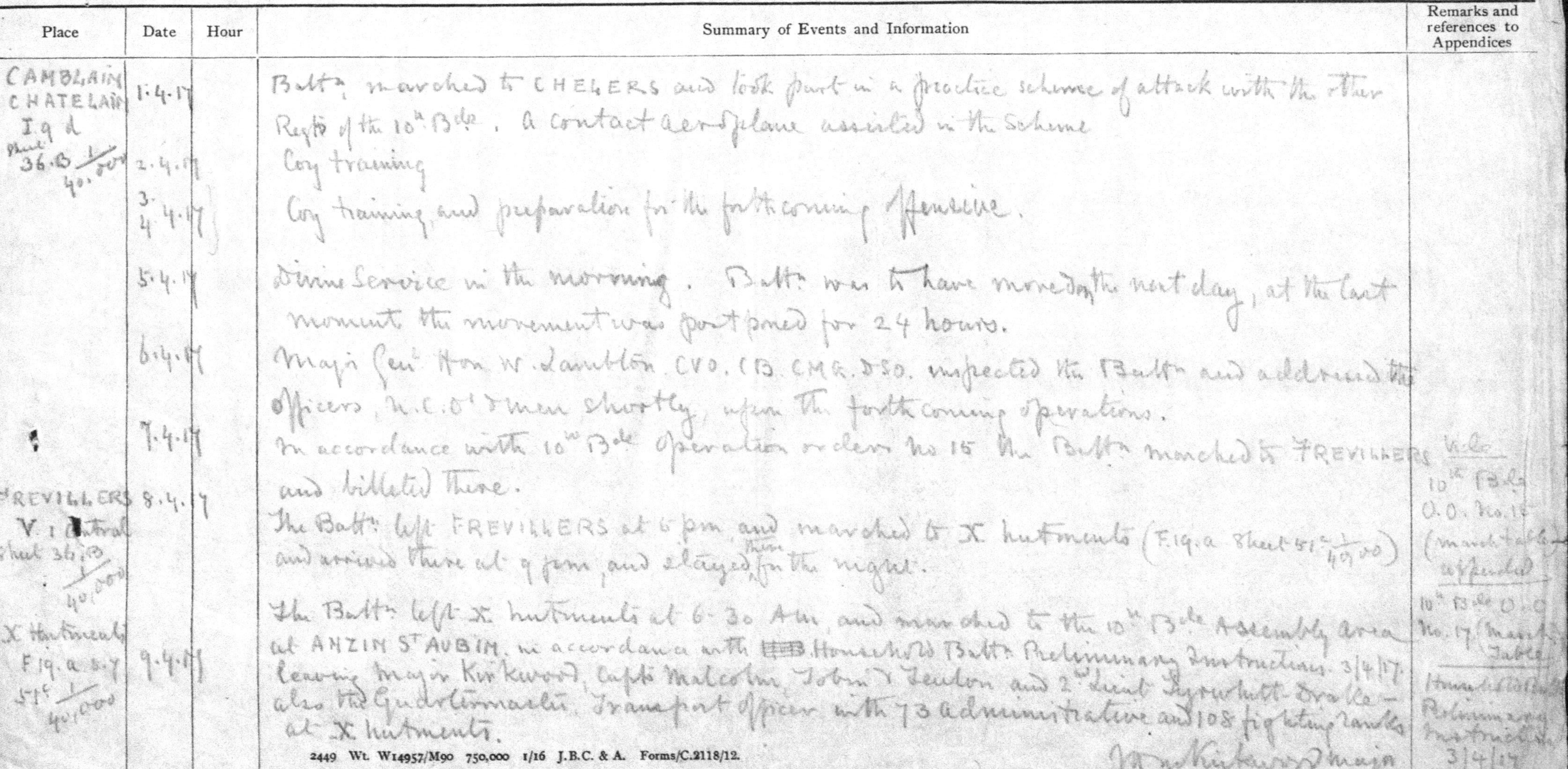

Instructions regarding War Diaries and Intelligence Summaries are contained in F. S. Regs., Part II. and the Staff Manual respectively. Title Pages will be prepared in manuscript.

WAR DIARY
or
INTELLIGENCE SUMMARY
(Erase heading not required.)

Army Form C. 2118.

Place	Date	Hour	Summary of Events and Information	Remarks and references to Appendices
CAMBLAIN CHATELAIN I.9.d Sheet 36.B 1/40,000	1.4.17		Battn. marched to CHELERS and took part in a practice scheme of attack with the other Regts of the 10th Bde. A contact aeroplane assisted in the scheme	
	2.4.17		Coy training	
	3. 4.4.17		Coy training and preparation for the forthcoming offensive.	
	5.4.17		Divine Service in the morning. Battn. was to have moved on the next day, at the last moment the movement was postponed for 24 hours.	
	6.4.17		Major Genl. Hon W. Lambton CVO. CB. CMG. DSO. inspected the Battn. and addressed the officers, N.C.O's & men shortly, upon the forthcoming operations.	
	7.4.17		In accordance with 10th Bde. operation orders No 15 the Battn. marched to FREVILLERS and billeted there.	Vide 10th Bde. O.O. No. 15
FREVILLERS V.1 Central Sheet 36.B 1/40,000	8.4.17		The Battn. left FREVILLERS at 6 pm and marched to X. hutments (F.19.a Sheet 51c 1/40,000) and arrived there at 9 pm, and stayed there for the night.	(march table appended)
X Hutments F.19.a 5.7 51c 1/40,000	9.4.17		The Battn. left X. hutments at 6-30 AM, and marched to the 10th Bde. Assembly area at ANZIN ST AUBIN, in accordance with Household Battn. Preliminary Instructions 3/4/17. Leaving Major Kirkwood, Capts Malcolm, Tobin & Fenton and 2nd Lieut Tyrwhitt-Drake – also the Quartermaster, Transport officer with 73 administrative and 108 fighting ranks at X. hutments.	10th Bde O.O. No. 17 (March Table). Household Battn. Preliminary Instructions 3/4/17

J. M. Kirkwood Major

2449 Wt. W14957/M90 750,000 1/16 J.B.C. & A. Forms/C.2118/12.

Instructions regarding War Diaries and Intelligence Summaries are contained in F. S. Regs., Part II. and the Staff Manual respectively. Title Pages will be prepared in manuscript.

WAR DIARY or INTELLIGENCE SUMMARY

(Erase heading not required.)

Army Form C. 2118.

Place	Date	Hour	Summary of Events and Information	Remarks and references to Appendices
ANZIN ST AUBIN V BLUE LINE H.J. d85 French Map	9.4.17 (Contd)		The Battn then carried out the scheme of work laid down in Household Battn Preliminary Instruction 3/4/17	
	10.4.17		Carrying work etc continued up to the BROWN and GREEN lines following out the above instructions	appended
	11.4.17 12.4.17		The narrative of operations of Household Battn 11/4/17 – 12/4/17 embodies the operations for these two days.	Narrative of H. Bn Operations 11/4/17–12/4/17
	13.4.17		The Battn moved back to the BLUE LINE and occupied dug-outs there.	10th Inf. Bde O.O. No 18 & 19
			The following were the casualties for the operations of 9/4/17 – 12/4/17:–	
			Officers — Killed: Capt C.H. Boddington; A.P. Godfrey	
			Died of Wounds: 2nd Lieut V.A. Bolitho	
			Wounded: " " K.A. Campbell — Total 4. Officers	
			O.R — Killed: 31	
			Died of Wounds: 5	
			Wounded: 124	
			Missing (believed killed): 5	
			Missing: 1	
			Total 166 O.R	

[signature] Major

2449 Wt. W14957/M90 750,000 1/16 J.B.C. & A. Forms/C.2118/12.

Army Form C. 2118.

Instructions regarding War Diaries and Intelligence Summaries are contained in F. S. Regs., Part II. and the Staff Manual respectively. Title Pages will be prepared in manuscript.

WAR DIARY
or
INTELLIGENCE SUMMARY

(Erase heading not required.)

Place	Date	Hour	Summary of Events and Information	Remarks and references to Appendices
BLUE LINE A.7.d.8.5 Trench Map	14.4.17		The Battn moved back to dug-outs & shelters in the BLACK line.	
	15.4.17		The day was spent in cleaning up arms & clothing as far as was possible	appendices
BLACK Line.	16.4.17		The Battn relieved the 1st East Lancashire Regt. v. Household Battn O.O. No 5. 16/4/17 the following officers being left behind. Capt. Pelly, 2nd Lieut Pym. & 2nd Lieuts Sandford & Bower	H.B. O.O. No 5 16.4.17
G.12.a.7.b Trench Map			Owing to the fact that the guides were not at the rendez-vous at the hour laid down & that they were unable to find their way up to the front line Companys, the relief was not completed until 4-25 AM.	
	17.4.17		The dispositions were as follows:- Frontage (H11.b6.9 — H5b45). Royal Irish Fusiliers on right Naval Division on the left	
H.11.a.6.2 Trench Map 51B NW 1/20,000			No. 2. Coy. on right of the line: 2 advanced posts of 1 platoon each; 2 support " " " "	
			No 1 Coy on the left.: 1 advanced post held by 1 platoon; 2 strong points in support each held by 1 platoon; 1 Platoon at Coy HQrs	
			No. 3 Coy in Support at EFFIE TRENCH. (H9d42)	
			No 4 Coy for carrying purposes, also in EFFIE TRENCH.	
			Battn H.Q with No 2. Coy in Sunken road at H.11a6 2	
			[signature] Major	

Army Form C. 2118.

Instructions regarding War Diaries and Intelligence Summaries are contained in F. S. Regs., Part II. and the Staff Manual respectively. Title Pages will be prepared in manuscript.

WAR DIARY
or
INTELLIGENCE SUMMARY

(Erase heading not required.)

Place	Date	Hour	Summary of Events and Information	Remarks and references to Appendices
H11 a 6.2 French Maps Sheet 51B NW 1/20,000	18.4.17		The 2nd Battn Seaforth Highlands having furnished a working party to dig posts in our advance line. No I Coy occupied one of these in the early hours of the morning and we then held 4 ~~posts~~ advance posts instead of 3. Captn Malcolm was slightly wounded by a sniper, & Captn Fenton took over No I Coy. Patrols ~~[illegible]~~ went along the German wire, from each company.	
	19.4.17.		Heavy bombardment on both sides. At night a patrol under 2nd Lieut Barker occupied some German Anti-aircraft dug-outs close to the German front line, & established a post there.	
	~~[illegible]~~		Some interesting correspondence was obtained in them.	
	20.4.17.		Heavy bombardment intermittently. In the evening the Battn was relieved by the 10th Battn York & Lancaster Regt. The Relief went off well excepting for some casualties from shell fire on the way back. The Battn marched back to tents & dug-outs at G11.A. It was a long march back & some of the Coys were not in camp until 3-30 Am. Casualties from 16.4.17 – 20.4.17 – mostly from shell fire – were as follows:–	(63rd Inf Bde) 10th Inf Bde O.O. No 22 appended
			Officers wounded Captn P. Malcolm – Total 1 Officer	
			O.R Killed 4	
			~~Died of wounds~~	
			Wounded 22 Total 26 O.R	

2449 Wt. W14957/M90 750,000 1/16 J.B.C. & A. Forms/C.2118/12.

Instructions regarding War Diaries and Intelligence Summaries are contained in F. S. Regs., Part II. and the Staff Manual respectively. Title Pages will be prepared in manuscript.

WAR DIARY
or
INTELLIGENCE SUMMARY

(Erase heading not required.)

Army Form C. 2118.

Place	Date	Hour	Summary of Events and Information	Remarks and references to Appendices
	21st 4.17		The Batt left G.11 A at 3 p.m & went in motor busses to AMBRINES where they arrived about 9.30 p.m owing to the lorries being 3 hours late – Here the Batt was billeted in barns together with Bde H.Q & [illegible]	
	22nd 4.17		Sunday. ~~[illegible]~~ Reorganization of platoons & inspections of Kit. Draft of 188 in all. 1 off 2/Lt Grenhill – 2/Lt [illegible] arrived off Lewis Gun course.	
	23. 4.17		Coy Training.	
	24. 4.17		Route March via LIGNEREUIL – GIVENCHY-LE-NOBLE – VILLERS SUR SIMON	
	25. 4.17		Coy Training as laid down in scheme – Verification of casualties from 9th to 20th April show the following to have taken place in the [illegible] Batt. Officers: Killed 2, Died of Wounds 1, Wounded 2, Wounded believed Killed NIL, Missing –. O.R: Killed 33, Died of Wounds 5, Wounded 151 (5 at duty), Wounded believed Killed 11, Missing 1. 109 [illegible]	
	26. 4.17		Coy Training. Lecture by C.R.E. of [illegible] Div on "Consolidation".	
	27. 4.17		Coy Training. Draft of 1 officer 2/Lt G.D. Williams & 30 O.R. arrived – [illegible]	
	28th 4.17		Battn moved from AMBRINES to Y. Hutments (H.Q. [illegible] ARRAS road).	
	29th 4.17		Battn moved from Y Hutments to billets in ARRAS (NORTH of Town). Party of officers & 70 O.R. went to [illegible] who were not going into line.	
	30th		Battn [illegible] up [illegible] line & relieved 15th & 16th R. Scots & 10th Lincolns (101st Bde) taking over line on right subsector I 19 A 8.7 to H 24 D 9.2. No 3 Coy on left of line, 4 [illegible] on right, 1 & 2 in reserve. Officers in line. H.Q. Maj [illegible] (commanding), [illegible] D [illegible], 2/Lt Sandford, Capt [illegible] R.A.M.C., [illegible] (CHAPLAIN). No 1 Coy: Lt O.S. Postal, 2/Lt M. Grenhill, [illegible] A. Boyd. 2 Coy: Capt [illegible], 2/Lt [illegible], 2/Lt Barr, 2/Lt [illegible]. No 3 Coy: Capt Telly, 2/Lt [illegible], 2/Lt [illegible]. No 4 Coy: 2/Lt Waring, 2/Lt S [illegible], 2/Lt [illegible]	

7449 Wt. W14957/M90 750,000 1/16 J.B.C. & A. Forms/C.2118/12.

3/11/17.

Household Battn. Preliminary Instructions, 1

1 (a) DRESS. All Officers taking part in the forthcoming operation, will be dressed exactly as the men. Sticks will not be carried.

(b) All specialists & carrying parties will wear distinguishing marks in accordance with instructions. Only Officers & N.C.Os of A party (400 men & 8 Officers) will wear yellow bands.

2. (a) FIGHTING DRESS. The pack will not be carried but will be left behind in camp with all men's spare kit. Labels will be issued to attach to their packs.

(b) The Haversack will be carried on the back. An extra pair of socks to be carried. Waterproof sheet to be strapped on outside of Haversack. Only unexpired portion of 1 days ration together with Iron Ration will be carried.

(c) AMMUNITION. Every man will carry 170 rounds S.A.A., excepting Lewis Gunners who will carry 50 rounds, also Signallers & Runners.

(ii) Every man will carry 2 No. 5 Mills Grenades & 2 Sandbags (The Mills Grenades will be drawn at X Hutments, also Sandbags)

3. The Battalion will take their Lewis Guns with 5 carriers (i.e. 20 Magazines per gun) to the assembly area where they will be left there in L.G. Limbers under Lt Whitelaw.

4. Three cookers and two water carts will also be taken to the assembly area where they will remain under CPL of H.Q. TURNER.

5. "A" party (400 men & 8 Officers) will work under Divisional Instructions.
"B" party (100 men & 3 Officers) will work under the C.R.E.
No 3 party (18 men & 1 Officer) will carry for the 10th M.G. Coy.
CAPT. BODINGTON will command A party
CAPT. PELL " " B "
LIEUT. CAMPBELL " " No3 "

6. 25 Officers & 181 O.R. (including 73 Administrative) will remain at X Hutments under the Command of MAJOR KIRKWOOD.

3

Preliminary Instruction No 2.

1. Intention. (a)

The IV th Division will form part of the XVII th Corps and take part in the Operations of the 3rd Army.

The IV Division will be in reserve in rear of the IX Division.

The IV Division will pass through the IX Division capture the II German trench System and the village of FAMPOUX and establish itself on the Green line. The XII Infantry Bgde will be on the right and the XI Infantry Bgde on the left.

The X Infantry Bgde will be in Divisional reserve. The role of the X th Infantry Bde is to take over consolidating the Brown line from the IX Division and be prepared to support either the XI or XII Infantry Bde.

(b) "A" and "B" carrying + working parties will be found in accordance with appendix attached.

2. (a) Preliminary Dispositions

On the evening of Y day the H.B will be concentrated in X Camp, 1000 yds south of ECOIVRES, near X roads F19 a 56.

(b) On Z day at zero plus 1·30 hour, H.B will be clear of X road F.19 a 56, and will move

to assembly area (See Map 'C').
[illegible] boards are being erected to show area for each Unit.

Route. X roads F 19 a 56 – X roads L 2 b 72 – across railway L 3 a 58 – road junction F 29 d 21 – across river F 27 a 60 – X roads F 27 d 61 – road junction F 28 c 11 – road junction L 14 a 74 – LOUEZ – ST. AUBIN – ANZIN – ST. AUBIN.

(c). Bde will remain assembly area till zero plus 6.30 hours during which period a hot meal will be given.

(d) Cookers, water carts, pack animals & 2 Lewis Gun limbers will be sent on ahead to assembly area.

Route. Road junction E 29 b 83 – main ARRAS road – X roads L 10 c 30 – LOUEZ – ST. AUBIN – ANZIN – ST. AUBIN.

(e) No 3 party will move at zero plus 6.45 hours from the assembly area and proceed in rear of I M.G. Coy. along the XII Bde southern track as far as the Blue line. Party 'A' will move on to the track at G 8 d 60 at zero plus 6.55 hours and proceed along XI Bde track as far as G 1 b 24 (25 yds between platoons). Party 'B' marching in rear of party E

5

(R.W. Regt) will pass G.8 d 60 at zero plus 6.59 hours & proceed along XII th Bde southern track to Rendezvous at H 7 d 90. Battalion H Qrs will proceed to the Blue Line. 103rd Inf Brig: will be prepared to move from the Assembly Area to support either the 34th or 51st Div: should the necessity arise. The Bttn carrying parties will be included in the strength of the working parties & will be available for work until called upon to go back for rations & water for their own party. Pack animals will be under Bttn. Orders.

Preliminary Instruction No 4.

4. Boundaries between Bdes:

~~Right bo~~ 12th Infantry Bde.

Right boundary - River SCARPE.

Left Boundary :- G16 central - G17 central north corner of cemetery in G18 central - bridge over railway cutting on Blue line at H8 c00 (to left Bde). - thence a line due E cutting the Brown line S of the trench junction at H9 c60, and 4th German trench system at H10 d70 - thence along the communication trench (inclusive to 12th Inf Bde) to road junction H17 a39. (11th Inf. Bde). - thence a straight line to the Green line at H12 c48.

11th Infantry Bde.

Right Boundary - as above.

Left Boundary - Bridge over railway S of the BOIS DE LA MAISON BLANCHE at H1 d30. - thence eastwards to point where the German trench meets the GAVRELLE road at H3 d24, thence a straight line to the NE corner of HYDERABAD REDOUBT at H12 a10

5. The Brown line will be consolidated by the 1st Bde

6.

6. Moves of Bde & Battn.

(a) On X day 6th April, Battn. moves to FREVILLERS and Bde to CHELLERS.

(b) On Y day Bde H.Qrs. & B Battn in X Camp.

(c) On Z day Zero hour Bde H.Q.s will be at G16 a 24 and they will move to G 17 a 2 3 4 8 before the Bde crosses the original British front line trench & will move later to FORRESTIER REDOUBT at G17 a 7845. (Positions of Div & Bde H.Qrs, dumps etc. are shown in appendix "A" and "B" attached.) Bttn H Qrs. will move to the Blue line N of where it cuts the GAVRELLE ROAD after the three working parties have left the assembly area and on arrival a runner will be sent to Bde H Q.s at G 17 a 2348 giving exact location.

7. The following maps will be carried:–
1/5,000 of Trench area, down to and including Platoon Commdrs. (vide instructions issued with these maps.)
1/20,000. Sheet 51 b N.W.
Other maps will be returned to Orderly Room

4.
(cont.). Attention is called to instructions to training of Divisions, para 33.

PARTY	STRENGTH		WORK		STORES	RENDEZ-VOUS		TOOLS + where drawn
OFFICERS.	OFF'S	O.R.	NATURE.	SITE		TIME	PLACE.	
Capt. [illegible] Lt. [illegible] " [illegible] " Bolitho " [illegible] " [illegible] " [illegible] " Bowers. "A" Party.	8	400	Carrying from G 16 b 2 4 to advanced DIV. DUMP. H. 13 b. 5.4. from there ½ to 11th Pole in Brown line H 9 a 9. b. ½ to 12th Pole in Brown line H 8 a b 5.2.	–	100 Bxs S.A.A. 200 Bxs Mills Bombs	Zero + 7 hrs	G 16 b 2 4	NIL.
"B" Party. Capt. [illegible] Lt. [illegible] " Moffatt	3	100	Repairing road from H 4 d 9.0 – H 9 a 2.7.	H.4 d. 9.0	NIL.	5.0 p.m.	H 4 d 9.0.	70 Shovels 30 picks drawn at Assembly Area
No. 3 Party Lt. Campbell	1	18	Carrying for 10th M.G. Coy.	BLUE LINE	NIL.			NIL.

"APPENDIX 'A'"

Appendix "B".

Position of Headquarters, Dumps etc.

1.		Railhead.	During Operations.	TINQUES.
2.	Headquarters.	44th Div: H.Q.	"Z" day.	ETRUN.
		" later.		G.17.a. 23.48.
		10th Brig: H.Q.	Zero hour.	G.8. a. 24.
		" " "	Before Bde crosses original British front line.	G.17.a. 23.48.
		" " "	As soon as DIVN. H.Q. move forward.	G.17.a. 70.45. Forrestier Redoubt
3.	Supplies.	Division Ration Dump. + reserve of water in tins	During Operations	Barn W of Oil Factory G.16. d. 9. 6.
		Water filling points.	" "	G.7. b. 6. 8. – (ANZIN) G.16. c. 67. ST. NICHOLAS.
4.	Ammunition.	Main Div. Dump.	" "	ST. NICHOLAS. G.16. c. 77.
		Advanced do.	" "	H.13. b. 84
		Bde Dump.	" "	Beside road running diagonally across Square H. 8.
5	R.E. Stores.	9th Div. Dump.	" "	ANZIN. G.7. b. 56.
		Advanced 9th Div Dump.	" "	ANZIN G.16. d. 37.
		Advanced Brig. Dump.	" "	ANZIN. H.9. a. 27. H.14. b. 81.

6. Medical.	Div. Walking wounded	During Operations	(near ST. LAURENT BLANGY.
	Advanced Dressing Stn.	" "	(Near Rly. Embankment (or ATHIES or (L'ABBAYETTE – (H.14. b. 8·3.
	9th Div. do.	" "	ST. NICHOLAS. G.16. c 58.
7. Salvage.	Corps salvage dumps.	" "	MAROEUIL & AUBIGNY.
	Divn. " "	" "	X roads G.16. d. 58.
	Advanced " "	" "	H. 13. b. 35.
8. Prisoners of War.			
	Divn. Collecting Post.	" "	G.15. b. 91.
	Advanced. do.	" "	L'ABBAYETTE. H.14. b. 83.

-SECRET-
****

Copy No...1.....

10TH INFANTRY BRIGADE OPERATION ORDER NO.15.

Ref.LENS Sheet 1/100,000. 5th April 1917.

1. The 10th Infantry Brigade Group will march to CHELERS area tomorrow, 6th inst. in accordance with attached march table.

2. The following distances will be kept on the line of march -

Between Coys. 200 yards.
" Battalions 400 yards.
" Transport of Units. 200 yards.

3. First line Transport will accompany units.

4. Advance billeting parties will meet Staff Captain in their respective villages at the Mairie by 10a.m. at latest.

5. Brigade H.Q. will close at OURTON at 10.30a.m. and reopen at CHELERS on arrival.

6. Units will report their arrival in billets to Brigade H.Q., and number of men, if any, who fell out on the line of march.

7. Acknowledge.

H.G.L. Fellowes
Captain B.M.
10th Infantry Brigade.

Issued at 12 noon.

Copy No. 1 to Household Battalion.
2 1st R.Warwick Regt.
3 2nd Seaforth Highrs.
4 1st R.Irish Fusrs.
5 10th M.Gun Company.
6 12th Field Ambce.
7 No.2 Coy. Train.
8 4th Div. Train.
9 Staff Captain.
10 Asst. Staff Captain.

No. 11 to 4th Division "G".
12 -do- "Q".
13 11th Inf. Brigade.
14 12th Inf. Brigade.
15 C.R.E.
16 A.D.M.S.
17 A.D.V.S.
18 A.P.M.
19 D.A.D.O.S.
20 Bde Transport Officer.

21 to Bde Signalling Officer.
22 War Diary.
23 -do-
24 File.
25 B.M.
26 10th Fd. Amb.

March Table to Accompany 10th Inf.Brigade Operation Order No.15.

*****

Unit.	From.	To.	Starting Point.	Time.	Route.	Remarks.
1st R.Irish Fus.	DIEVAL.	X Huts.	S.W.exit of DIEVAL.	9.15a.m.	Junction of DIEVAL-ST.POL and LA THIEULOYE-VALHOUN roads-LA THIEULOYE-MONCHY BRETON-CHELERS-TINQUES-SAVY-main ARRAS Rd- Road Junction on main road 1 mile due South of 1st C in CHINCY, east of HAUTE AVESNES.	Follow in rear of No.3 Coy.Train, 11th Brigade. Pass line CHELERS-FREVILLERS by 11.45a.m.
No.2 Coy. Train.	OURTON.	GUESTREVILLE	S.exit of OURTON.	10.15a.m.	LA COMTE-HOUVELIN- FREVILLERS.	
10th M.Gun Company.	OURTON.	CHELERS.	S.exit of OURTON.	10.25a.m.	LA COMTE-MAGNICOURT- Road junction 1 mile due S.W.of MAGNICOURT.	
Brigade H.Q.	OURTON.	CHELERS	-do-	10.35a.m.	-do-	
2nd Seaforth Highrs.	OURTON.	VILLERS-BRULIN.	-do-	10.45a.m.	LA COMTE-HOUVELIN-FREVILLERS.	
12th Field Ambce.	OURTON.	CHELERS.	-do-	11a.m.	LA COMTE-MAGNICOURT-Road Junction 1 mile due S.W. of MAGNICOURT.	
1st R.Warwick Regt.	CAMBLAIN-CHATELAIN.	BETHONSART.	Cross Rds ½mile due W.of STA. CALONNE-RICOUART.	~~9.55~~a.m. 10.10	OURTON-LA COMTE-HOUVELIN-FREVILLERS.	
Household Bn.	-do-	FREVILLERS.	-do-	10.30a.m.	OURTON-LA COMTE-HOUVELIN.	

-S E C R E T-
************   Copy No. 1.........

10TH INFANTRY BRIGADE OPERATION NO. 17.

Ref.LENS Sheet 1/100,000.   6th April 1917.

1. The 10th Inf. Brigade Group (less 1st R.Irish Fus.) will move from CHELERS area to X huts on April 8th, in accordance with attached march table.

2. Companies will march closed up, with 400 yards between battalions.
   1st line Transport will accompany units.

3. The following advanced parties will report to Staff Captain, at Camp Commandant's Office, Camp X at 11.30a.m. on 8th April.

   (a) Quartermaster or Regt.Q.M.S. and 5 O.R's per Battn., Qr Mr Sgt. and 2 O.R. from M.Gun Coy, to take over rations for next days consumption.

   (b) 2 N.C.O's and 6 men per Battn to take over pack saddles, grenades etc.
   Three of these men should be able to assemble the saddles

   Those parties are in addition to any others detailed in previous Administrative Orders.

4. Brigade H.Q. will close at CHELERS at 5.30p.m. and reopen at Camp X at 6.30p.m.

5. Units will report their arrival in Camp to Brigade H.Q.

6. Acknowledge.

[signature]
Captain B.M.
10th Infantry Brigade.

Issued at 8p.m.

Copy No.		No.	
1	to Household Battalion.	13	to 11th Inf. Brigade.
2	1st R.Warwick Regt.	14	12th Inf. Brigade.
3	2nd Seaforth Hrs.	15	C.R.E.
4	1st R.Irish Fusrs.	16	A.D.M.S.
5	10th M.Gun Coy.	17	A.D.V.S.
6	12th Fd Ambulance.	18	A.P.M.
7	No.2 Coy. Train.	19	D.A.D.O.S.
8	4th Div. Train.	20	Bde Transport Officer.
9	Staff Captain.	21	Bde Signalling Officer.
10	Asst.Staff Captain.	22	War Diary.
11	4th Division "G".	23	-do-
12	-do- "Q".	24	File
		25	B.M.
		26	10th Fd. Amb.

March Table to accompany 10th Brigade Operation Order No.17.

****

Unit.	From.	To.	Starting Point.	Time.	Route.	Remarks.
No.2 Coy.Train.	GUESTREVILLE.	X Camp.	Church in VILLERS-BRULIN.	5.30p.m.	VILLERS-BRULIN - SAVY - main ARRAS Road - Rd. Junc. 1 mile S. of 1st C in CHINCY, east of HAUTE-AVESNES.	
2nd Seaforth Hrs.	VILLERS-BRULIN.	-do-	-do-	5.40p.m.	-do-	
1st R.Warwick Regt.	BETHONSART.	-do-	Church in BETHONSART.	5.50p.m.	SAVY-thence as above.	From Savy in rear of 2nd Seaforth Highrs.
Household Bn.	FREVILLERS.	-do-	Church in FREVILLERS.	5.25p.m.	VILLERS-BRULIN - SAVY - thence as above.	From Savy in rear of 1st R.Warwickshire R.
Brigade H.Q.	CHELERS.	-do-	Railway Crossing over CHELERS-TINQUES Rd.	5.35p.m.	TINQUES-SAVY-thence as above.	From Savy in rear of Household Battalion.
10th M.Gun Coy.	CHELERS.	-do-	-do-	5.45p.m.	-do-	
10th Fd.Ambce.	CHELERS.	-do-	-do-	5.55p.m.	-do-	
12th Fd.Ambce.	CHELERS.	-do-	-do-	6.5p.m.	-do-	

Narration of Operations of Household Battn. 11/4/17 – 12/4/17.

[illegible] was sent for to Brigade HQ by [illegible] Brigade [illegible] orders No 12 [illegible] [illegible]

The H.B. paraded at 7.15 A.M. [illegible] [illegible] in CAVALRY ROAD [illegible] Dump to pick up grenades, flares.
They arrived at the [illegible] H 17 [illegible] at 9.45 AM.
I waited in the FAMPOUX ROAD to see O.C. Seaforths as I was to follow him at Zero + 2 i.e. 2 p.m. I saw him, & O.C. Royal Irish Fusiliers.
At 10.45 A.M. an officer brought me a note from the 10th Brigade Major saying that Zero hour was to start at Zero + 10 minutes instead of Zero + 2 hours. The message stated that we were to leave our start so as to reach the final objective at Zero + 40 min, which meant starting at Zero + 10 minutes.
I showed the order to O.C. Royal Irish Fusiliers Regiment who was with me & then sent to my company commanders as I barely had time to get up to the 2nd Assembly Area, for i.e. HB [illegible] from HYDERABAD REDOUBT – TRENCH crossing road at H 17 B.6.9.
I went with No 4 Co. my left Co. into FAMPOUX No 1 in the centre following, then No 3 which

made from the right. As we went through FAMPOUX I met O.C. Essex Regiment who told me to hurry my men through as it had been shelled heavily the night before. I dropped back & came along with my right Co. When I got to the fork ROADS in FAMPOUX I found my two leading Companies had gone to the left to work up the trenches to the assembly area, as the other road was under heavy machine gun fire. It was then 11.55.

At Zero hour the Germans put down a very heavy barrage on the forked ROADS & ~~the [illegible]~~ FAMPOUX itself.

No 4 Co. worked along the HUMID & HAVSACK TRENCH to the HYDERABAD REDOUBT. No 2 Company my support Company along HUMID TRENCH & the ROAD, followed by No 3 Company.

At Zero + 10 minutes the three Companies started in a very heavy barrage & machine gun fire.

The leading two companies | No 4 were leading as they had to get out singly from HYDERABAD REDOUBT, the company commander & ~~three~~ ~~2 platoons were practically~~ was killed and the two platoons practically destroyed at once.

The ~~rest~~ two other platoons after losing heavily were collected & brought into the HYDERABAD REDOUBT by 2 Lieut Le Wadlyn.

No 2 Co. also lost heavily, Lieut Godfrey being killed immediately, & Lieut Campbell severely wounded, 2nd Lieut Buchanan brought them back & reorganised them in the sunken road.

No 3 Company under Captain Pelly kept their right as far as possible in touch with the Royal Warwickshire Regiment & had his right resting in HUDDLE TRENCH.

In the meantime I moved my Hdqtrs from the X Roads H 17 B 6.0 – H 17 B 9.0

At 2.30 PM I received a message from my right company commander telling me of the position he had been obliged to take up. At 5 PM Capt Pelly came to see me in FAMPOUX. I told him to consolidate the position as far as possible. I then moved back to H 17 C 2 6.

At 6 PM I got into communication with O.C. R.I.F & O.C. R.W.R & we discussed the situation. It was then arranged that I should move what remained of my left & centre companies into HUDDLE TRENCH & be responsible with a small party of the R.W.R. line as far as H 18 A 9 9 with No 3 Company in support in the SUNKEN ROAD. This was immediately done. I also got into communication with O.C. Seaforths at HYDERABAD REDOUBT. At 11 AM on 12th my Headquarter Dug out was blown in and I moved to H 17 C 7 6. At 4.30 PM the 9th Division lined up & attacked from the SUNKEN ROAD in which my Headquarters were, & immediately the Germans put a heavy barrage down. The 9th Div. suffered very heavily & many of them got into the German trenches on my left, but were withdrawn that evening. At 7 PM I was ordered to withdraw be relieved by 9th Division which owing to their losses they were unable to do. At 7 AM 13th I sent to the Brigade for further orders. I was told to withdraw, and I withdrew the Batt at 7.45 A.M., having lost roughly about 180 casualties.

[illegible]

Lieut Colonel

Commanding HOUSEHOLD Bn

Secret

10th Infantry Bde. O.O. No 18

11th April 1917

1. 4th Division will advance today 11th April and secure ~~line~~ PLOUVAIN – GREEN LAND HILL – INN I.7.a.3.8 – HYDERABAD REDOUBT.
The attack will be carried out by 12th, 10th and 11th Bdes in this order from South to North.

2. 1st Objective. ROEUX – GAVRELLE RD. and defensive flank from INN to HYDERABAD REDOUBT.
2nd Objective. PLOUVAIN – GREENLAND HILL and defensive flank thence to INN.

3. Boundaries.
10th Brigade Right Boundary.
Chateau I13d21 – HAUSA WOOD (exclusive) – PLOUVAIN (inclusive).
Left Boundary.
PLOUVAIN inclusive – GREENLAND HILL pt. I7b07 – road to FAMPOUX exclusive.

4. Preliminary Moves.

S.A. Brigade will relieve Seaforths and Irish Fusrs. in Brown Line by 7 a.m.

These two battalions will then move to Area due W. of FAMPOUX and be in position there by 10 am.

Seaforths will keep North of FAMPOUX – ATHIES Rd and will not go beyond Sunken Road from H17c 25 to H16 b 80.

Irish Fusrs will keep S. of FAMPOUX – ATHIES Road and not enter village.

At 10 am. Seaforths will advance in fours down road to Cross-roads H.17 d 5½ 8½ – thence up Sunken road to HYDERABAD REDOUBT, their rear to be where trench crosses Sunken road at H17 b 69 and will form up for attack.

At 10-10 a.m Irish Fus. will follow in rear of Seaforths up same Sunken road as far as where trench crosses road at H17 b 69 and their rear to be at H17 b 62 and will form up for attack

4. cont.

Both Battalions to be in position there by 11 a.m.

When first 2 battalions of SA Brigade have passed Railway Cutting (Blue Line), Household Bn and Warwicks will advance and form up in rear of Seaforths and Irish Fusrs. respectively.

At Zero hour, when Seaforths and Irish Fusrs. advance from Sunken Road, Household Battn. will advance to Sunken Road by same route and Warwicks will advance at Zero + 10 minutes ditto, both forming up for attack.

5. The Attack

(a) At Zero hour which is 12 noon Seaforths will advance on a 3 Coy. front and capture their objective from Cross roads I13a93 exclusive to Cross Rds I7a43 exclusive.

(b) Irish Fusrs will advance at Zero hour, 12 noon and capture their objective on a 2 coy. front from Cross Rds I13a93 inclusive to Chateau I13d21. (inclusive.

5. (cont)

Their 3rd Coy. will advance in rear of 2 front Coys. as far as present Green Line on E. edge of FAMPOUX and remain in reserve.

(c) At Zero plus 2 hours Household Battn. will advance from assembly area to their objective on a 3 coy. front, and will have to left wheel, objective from Cross Rds I7a43 up road exclusive to I7b07 thence GREENLAND HILL to Railway Embankment I9d36. This line must be held by a chain of posts from 200 yds to 250 yds apart.

(d) At Zero + 2 hours Warwicks will advance from Assembly Area to their objective on a 2 Coy. front: objective PLOUVAIN from Railway embankment I9d36 – E. edge of PLOUVAIN – S.E. edge of Wood I16a51.

The 3rd Coy. will advance in rear of 1st 2 coys and halt on line Station I9c63 to I15b80 and consolidate this line.

5. cont.

(e) 1 Section, M.G. Coy will advance with 1st R. Irish Fusils to 1st Objective and on reaching there will open fire on PLOUVAIN until Warwicks pass the 1st Objective.

2 Sections will advance with Household Battn and establish guns on GREENLAND HILL to fire N. & E.

1 Section will advance with Warwicks.

The Section with Warwicks will be the one from POINT DU JOUR which will be relieved by S. Africans at 7 a.m.

(f) ½ T. M. Battery will advance ~~with Household Bn [illegible]~~ with Warwicks.

Until ammunition arrives these men will be under orders of O.C. Battns for any work at the objective.

(g) All units will consolidate their positions immediately on capture of objective.

(h) In the case of all battalions the 4th coy. will do the carrying of S.A.A. & grenades.

6. Boundaries between Battns.
Trench across sunken road H17b69 – Cross roads I13a93 – railway embankment to I9d36 to Warwicks

7. Grenades & S.A.A.
Seaforths will draw from Dump at H9a17
Irish Fusrs from H15d33.
Household Bn. from Adv. Div. Dump at H13b55
Warwicks ditto

30 boxes S.AA and 40 boxes Mills grenades should be taken by each Bn. in addition to grenades carried by bombing sections.

8. Artillery
There will be a creeping barrage from Zero hour up to 1st Objective.* After this heavies will deal with PLOUVAIN and creeping barrage will move to line PLOUVAIN – GREENLAND HILL, parallel with 1st Objective.

100 in 2 minutes

8: cont.

The whole operation will not be delayed by any small parties of enemy there may be. Such parties must be boldly attacked and outflanked.

Boldness and energy are required. All platoon leaders to be told this.

9. Signals.

O.C. 10th Bde Signal Section will establish Visual Station near Bde HQ and also one on high ground due N. of ATHIES.

Household Bn. will establish one on GREENLAND HILL.

Seaforths one on high ground due E. of HYDERABAD REDOUBT

Warwicks will communicate with Household Bn. Station, who will communicate with Seaforths thence back to Bde Stns.

Inst Sns to Seaforths.

[signature]
Captain
Bde Major, 10th Bde

Issued at 2-15 am

SECRET

Copy No. 1.

10th Infy. Bde. Operation Order No. 19.

Ref. ARRAS Sheet 1/10,000
"FAMPOUX" 1/10,000

April 13th 1917.

1. The 4th Division will hold present front with one Brigade, the 11th Infy Bde.

2. The 10th Infy Bde. will move tomorrow 14th inst. to following areas:-
(a) Household Bn. - trenches in G 12 a + b.
2nd Seaforth Hdrs. - do - G 12 c + d.
in both cases exclusive of original British Front line.
If there is accommodation in trenches E. of these squares battalions may extend as far E. as H.7. central.
Suitable Bn. H.Q. for 2nd Seaforths is at G 12 d 84 approx. recently occupied by South African Brigade.
(b) 1st R. Warwickshire R. - trenches + cutting in Square H 7 a.
1st R. Irish Fusrs. - trenches + cutting in Square H.7.b.
(c) Bde. H.Q. at approx. H 7 d 93
(d) Trench shelters will be available to supplement accommodation + will be distributed tomorrow.

2.

3. All above moves to be completed by 12 noon, 14th inst.

4. Reinforcements, i.e. 108 men left behind will join battalions tomorrow.

5. If 1st R. Irish Fusrs. cannot find suitable dugouts for Bn. HQ, 1st R. Warwickshire R. will hand over dugout accommodation if possible in northern sector of their area.

6. Units will report when they are in their new area & position of Bn. HQ.

7. Each Bn. will send on an Officer and suitable party to reconnoitre their area previous to their battalions arrival

8. ACKNOWLEDGE.

[signature]
Captain B.M.
10th Infy Brigade

Issued at 8 p.m.

MESSAGES AND SIGNALS. No. of Message

Prefix ... Code ... m. | Words | Charge | This message is on a/c of: ... Service. | Recd. at ... m.
Office of Origin and Service Instructions. | Sent At ... m. To ... By ... | (Signature of "Franking Officer.") | Date ... From ... By ...

TO O.C. /

Sender's Number.	Day of Month.	In reply to Number.	AAA
*	16/4/17.		

Household Bn. Operation Orders No. 5.

1. Bn. will relieve 1st E. LANCASHIRE Regt in Left sub-sector (H5b4.5 – H11b6.9) to-night.

2. Parade ~~6.30~~ 7 p.m

3. Order of March. 1 Coy. 2 Coy. 3 Coy. 4 Coy. Bn H.Q. 100 yards between platoons.

4. Route POINT DU JOUR – road junction H3d0.0.

5. Guides will meet platoons at 9 p.m at H9a8.4. where LOCUST Trench cuts road.

6. Brigade Headquarters H9c4.0
Battn. " H9d6.8.

7. (a) Blankets rolled in bundles of 10 & taken to cookers – 2 p.m.
(b) Great-coats rolled in 5s taken to cookers 2 p.m.
No 766 Tpr. CROWLEY will be i/c of Dump.

From
Place
Time

The above may be forwarded as now corrected. (Z)
Censor. Signature of Addressor or person authorised to telegraph in his name.

* This line should be erased if not required.

750,000. W 2186 – M509. H. W. & V., Ld. 6/16.

(In pads of 100).
No. of Message

MESSAGES AND SIGNALS.

Prefix .... Code .... m. | Words | Charge

Office of Origin and Service Instructions.

Sent
At .... m.
To ....
By ....

* *This message is on a/c of:*
.... *Service.*
(Signature of "Franking Officer.")

Recd. at .... m.
Date ....
From ....
By ....

TO

Sender's Number.	Day of Month.	In reply to Number.	AAA
*	16/4/17		

8. All water-bottles to be carried full.

9. Completion of relief to be wired using code-word SANDY.

10. ACKNOWLEDGE

Issued at 9.45 a.m.
16/4/17

R. L. Bell
Lieut. & Adjt.

From
Place
Time

The above may be forwarded as now corrected.
(Z)

Censor. Signature of Addressor or person authorised to telegraph in his name.

* This line should be erased if not required.

750,000. W 2186–M509. H. W. & V., Ld. 6/16.

-SECRET-   Copy No.........

10TH INFANTRY BRIGADE OPERATION ORDER NO.22.

Ref. Sheet 51b N.W. 1/20,000.
LENS 1/100,000.   20th April 1917.

1. The 10th Inf. Bde. will be relieved in the line by the 63rd Inf. Bde. tonight 20th/21st April in accordance with attached table, and will move into Reserve Brigade Area and remain there till 4p.m. tomorrow, 21st inst., when the Brigade will proceed by bus to the HARBACQ area.

2. Guides from each unit will be sent to the rendezvous in charge of an officer, who will report to Brigade H.Q. on arrival

3. 10th M.Gun Coy. will be temporarily at the disposal of 37th Div. and will not move.

4. All trench stores, S.A.A., grenades etc. will be handed over to incoming units, a receipt obtained and forwarded to Brigade H.Q. by 4p.m. 21st inst.

5. All Point du Jour maps and aeroplane photographs will be handed over and a receipt obtained and forwarded to Brigade H.Q. as in para. 4 above.

6. Completion of relief will be reported by wire to Brigade H.Q. using BAB Code.

7. On completion of relief G.O.C. 10th Inf. Bde. will hand over command of the sector to G.O.C. 63rd Inf.Bde.

8.(a) Brigade H.Q. will close at present position on completion of relief and reopen at S.A.HQ, G.17.a.2348 on arrival. South African HQ.

(b) Each unit will send a runner to Brigade H.Q. at G.17.a.2348. at 8a.m. 21st giving location of Battalion H.Q.

9. Rations tonight will be delivered at old Divisional Dump West of Oil Factory.

10. Acknowledge.

H.G.L. Fellowes
Captain B.M.
10th Infantry Brigade.

Issued at 11.30 am.

Copy No.	To	No.	To
1	Household Battn.	17	O.C.Det.11th M.G.Coy.
2	1st R.Warwickshire R.	18	O.C.Det.12th M.G.Coy.
3	2nd Seaforth Highrs.	19	Staff Captain.
4	1st R.Irish Fusrs.	20	No.2 Coy. Train.
5	10th M.Gun Coy.	21	4th Div. Train.
6	10th T.M.Battery.	22	A.D.M.S.
7	21st W.Yorks. Regt.	23	A.D.V.S.
8	9th Field Coy.R.E.	24	D.A.D.O.S..
9	12th Field Ambce.	25	C.R.E.
10	4th Division "G".	26	A.P.M.
11	-do- "Q"	27	Asst. Staff Captain.
12	11th Inf. Bde.	28	Bde.Transport Officer.
13	12th Inf. Bde.	29	Bde. Signalling Officer.
14	189th Inf.Bde.	30	War Diary.
15	153rd Inf.Bde.	31	-do-
16	63rd Inf. Bde.	32	File.

March Table to accompany 10th Inf.Bde.Operation Order No.22.

Unit.	Relieving Unit.	From.	To.	Guides. Time.	Guides. Rendezvous.	Remarks.
2nd Seaforth Highrs.	8th Bn. Somerset Light Infantry.	Support.	Reserve Bde.Area, position will be notified later.	7p.m.	Bde.HMQ. H.9.c.40.	via L'ABBAYETTE - LAURENT BLANGY.
Household Bn.	10th Bn.York & Lancaster R.	Left Sub-Sector.	-do-	9p.m.	-do-	-do-
10th T.M.Batty.	63rd T.M.Batty.	Trenches.	-do-	9.[illegible]pm.	-do-	-do- A 10th M.G.Coy. limber will be at Bde H.Q. for their 4 guns and take them to 1st line transport.
1st R.Irish F.	4th Bn. Middlesex Rgt.	Right Sub-Sector.	-do-	10p.m.	-do-	via L'ABBAYETTE-LAURENT BLANGY.
1st. R. Warwickshire R.	8th Bn. Lincoln R.	Support.	-do-	11p.m.	-do-	-do-
10thBde H.Q.	63rd Bde H.Q.	H.9.c.40.	South African dug-outs C.17.a.2348	-	-	-do-
9th Field Coy. R.E.	-	H.4.d.50.	Reserve Brigade area.	March immediately after dark.		-do-
1 section, 12th M.G.Coy.	1 section, 63rd M.G.Coy.	Present	-do-	9p.m.	Bde H.Q. H.9.c.40.	-do- A 10th M.Gun Coy. limber will be at Bde. H.Q. for these guns and take them to 1st line transport.
½ section, 12th M.G.Coy. (anti-aircraft)	½ section, 63rd M.G.Coy.	position.	-do-	9p.m.	-do-	
1 section, 11th M.G.Coy. (anti-aircraft)	1 section, 63rd M.G.Coy.	H.15.c&d.	-do-	9p.m.	-do-	A 10th M.G.Coy. limber will be at cross roads H.15.a.00 for their guns.

Confidential

War Diary of

Household Battalion

for month of May 1917

Volume 7.

W.W. Wortel

Lieut-Colonel

Commanding

Household Battalion

Instructions regarding War Diaries and Intelligence Summaries are contained in F. S. Regs., Part II. and the Staff Manual respectively. Title pages will be prepared in manuscript.

WAR DIARY
or
INTELLIGENCE SUMMARY.
(Erase heading not required.)

Army Form C. 2118.

Place	Date	Hour	Summary of Events and Information	Remarks and references to Appendices
May 1st 1917			Battn in line I 19 A.8.7. to H 24 D.9.2. Day quiet – Work continued on deepening front line trench – Seven posts started about 50 yds in front of Front Line Trench – 8 of which were occupied. Snipers were active & bursts of machine gun fire swept our parapet intermittently throughout the night	Ref MAP FAMPOUX 51B N.W. 4
	2nd			
	3rd		Battn took part in general attack of 1st Div. Generalities. No 1 & 3 Coy to take 1st & 2nd objectives i.e. Black Line & Blue; junction Black Line & Roeux – Plouvain Rd. Attack on 2 Coy front. Inter coy boundary I 19 A 8.6. I 19 B. 3.5. to junction. No 3 Coy on left. No 1 on right. No 2 Coy 2 platns moppers up. 2 plats to form a defensive flank on right in case S.R.T. did not succeed in taking village of ROEUX. No 4 Coy carrying Coy & in reserve H 24 D 8.9.	Ink Narrative attached –
		3.45 a.m.	Attack – Succeeded at first on left but right immediately hung up by machine gun fire – Darkness much hindered progress of attack – 2nd Lt Baker only officer left in line. Battn compelled to retire to original front line trench. 2nd Lt Wauklyn sent up with 50 to reorganize line. Casualties exceedingly heavy.	
		12.50	Battn took part in Bombing attack up CARONA TRENCH (I 19 B 7.7) in conjunction with patrol [illegible] of A.W.R & R.F.?. 9.30 p.m. Left subsection of line taken over from S.A. Infantry.	
	4th		Reorganization of line. Pioneers (W Yorks) assisted & a line of six posts were completed from I 19 C 7.5 to I 19 B 1.2 in line with West corner of CEMETERY.	
	5.		Very quiet: Sniping active at night. Posts deepened.	
	6.		3 a.m. Bombing attack by 2nd Lt Wauklyn on enemy listening posts I 19 C 6.85 after excellent reconnaissance by 2nd Lt Moffat – causing nervous retaliation along whole of line.	

A5834 Wt. W4973/M687 750,000 8/16 D. D. & L. Ltd. Forms/C.2118/13.

Instructions regarding War Diaries and Intelligence Summaries are contained in F. S. Regs., Part II. and the Staff Manual respectively. Title pages will be prepared in manuscript.

WAR DIARY
or
INTELLIGENCE SUMMARY.

(Erase heading not required.)

Army Form C. 2118.

Place	Date	Hour	Summary of Events and Information	Remarks and references to Appendices
May 7th			Relieved in line by R. I. Fusiliers. Batt^n came back to 4th German System H.22.A & B.	Same Map
			Batt^n reorganized into 5 Platoons. Col. Portal [?] arrived at Transport.	
	8th		Batt^n rested.	
	9th		Batt^n proceeded up line to original position in front line. Batt^n H.Q. at Crum [?] Trench (H.24.D.8.9)	
	10th		Batt^n occupy left of original front line. East corner of Mt Pleasant WOOD (I.19.A.9.1.) trenches PELVIN [?] & first line.	
	11th		Batt^n took part in attack on CEMETERY 7.30 p.m. Objective [illegible] in East of N. end of village.	
			Officers Capt Tolmie [?] – 1 Plat. 2/Lt Buchanan [?] 2 Plat. 2/Lt Rice 3 Plat. 2/Lt Stockwood 4 Plat. 2/Lt Whalley [?] – right to left	
			H.Q. Major Kirkwood [?]. 2/Lt Dill-Cazalet – Sandford – Capt Sloane R.A.M.C.	vide Narrative [?]
			Attack successful. Seaforths moving up in rear of Batt^n. R.I.F. on right – R.W.[?] in reserve.	
			Casualties again very heavy. 2/Lt Stockwood only officer in line.	
	12		Batt^n relieved by 1/5th Seaforths & proceeded to Blue Line (H.13.B.9.4).	
	13		Batt^n proceeded in motor buses to HOUVIN - HOUVIGNEUL (2.3 central ref Lens 1/100000)	
	14		2nd [?] detachment arrived – original supplemented by 3 drafts 164 & 4 officers. 2/Lt Thomas, " Rogers, " Tune [?], " Blackburn	
			Gen Lambton (Div. Gen.) addressed Bde on recent successful operation.	[signature]

A5834 Wt. W4973/M687 750,000 8/16 D. D. & L. Ltd. Forms/C.2118/13.

Instructions regarding War Diaries and Intelligence Summaries are contained in F. S. Regs., Part II. and the Staff Manual respectively. Title pages will be prepared in manuscript.

WAR DIARY
or
INTELLIGENCE SUMMARY.
(Erase heading not required.)

Army Form C. 2118.

Place	Date	Hour	Summary of Events and Information	Remarks and references to Appendices
15.5.17			Memorial Service for Officers, N.C.Os & men who fell in action during the past month. April 9 – May 11.	[illegible]
16.5.17			Inspection & address by Army Commander (Gen Sir Edmund Allenby) – Brigade congratulated on their fine work.	
17.5.17			Specialist classes started.	
18.5.17			Batt. Parade & Training of Specialists – Regimental canteen [?] started. Draft of 1 Officer (2Lt Wakefield [?]) & 35 O.R.	
19.5.17			~~[illegible]~~ " Ditto "	
20.5.17			Church Parade.	
21.5.17			Batt. Parade – Specialist classes	
22.5.17			" Regimental Training started – Draft of 1 Officer (2Lt De Geijer) & 119 O.R.	
23.5.17			Physical Training – Batt. Parade – Specialists.	
24.5.17			" " 2Lt B.W. Gibbs arrived to rejoin	Orders [?] vide attached
25.5.17			Presentation Parade by Corps Commander.	
26.5.17			Batt. Training – 2 p.m. Brigade Sports.	
27.5.17			Church Parade. Lecture by Div Intelligence officer to all Officers N.C.Os & section leaders. 2Lt J.R.T. Burchell [?] joined unit	
28.5.17			Batt. Parade. Route March to Training Area at LIENCOURT.	
29.5.17			Organization of Specialist classes	
		9 p.m.	Night scheme. Practise attack & consolidation.	
30.5.17			Batt. Parade & Specialist Training. Lecture for all officers [illegible] Bayonet fighting.	
31.5.17			Batt. Parade	[signature illegible]

A5834 Wt. W4973/M687 750,000 8/16 D. D. & L. Ltd. Forms/C.2118/13.

HOUSEHOLD BATTALION

LIST OF AWARDS

153 Trooper Thomas Kay
Awarded the Military medal on the 28/5/17 for bravery at ROEUX ON 6/5/17

1177 Trooper R.J.Hamill
Awarded the MilitaryMedal on the 28/5/17 for bravery at ROEUX whilst acting as Platoon Runner

832 Tpr. (A/Cpl) Frederick Page
Awarded the Military Medal on the 28/5/17 for bravery whilst acting as signaller

14 Tpr. (A/Cpl of H) James W.Buckingham
Awarded the Military Medalon the 28/5/17 for bravery at ROEUX being the senior N.C.O. surviving 11/5/17

3028 Tpr. (A/Cpl.of H.) George E.Johnson
Awarded the Military Medal on the 28/5/17 for bravery at ~~FAMPOUX~~ ROUEX in charge of carrying party

553 Tpr.Alexande Westbrook
Awarded the Military Medal on the 28/5/17 for bravery at FAMPOUX whilst acting as Battn. H.Q. Runner

1547 A/Cpl. of Horse Walter Twidle
Awarded the Military Medal on the 15/5/17 for bravery at FAMPOUX on 11/4/17

6206 A/Cpl. of Horse Mayer
Awarded the Military Medal on the 25/5/17 for bravery at ROEUX as senior N.C.O. of the company

170 Tpr. Faithorn
Awarded the Military Medal on the 25/5/17 for bravery at ROEUX whilst acting as Stretcher Bearer

R.A.M.C. (attached Household Battalion)
Captain John Findlayson McGill Sloan
Awarded the Military Cross for bravery and dressing wounded under shell fire at FAMPOUX on 11/5/17

SECRET:–

1

10th Inf. Bde. O.O. No: 28

Ref. Biache Sheet 1/20,000 2nd May 1917

1(a) The 4th Div. will take part in a general attack by the Third Army on enemy position FRESNES-LES MONTABAN – PLOUVAIN.

(b) The VI Corps is attacking S. of River SCARPE + XIII Corps N. of XVIII Corps.

2. The 12th Bde. will attack on the left, 10th Bde. + 1 Bn. of 11th Bde. on right, 11th Bde. in support (less 1 Bn.)

3. Bde. N. Boundary. Cross Roads H18d 5510 – I13d15 – thence straight line to I16a00

Bde. S. Boundary River SCARPE

4. Objective 1 Black Line on map attached
" 2 Blue " " "
" 3 Red " " "

5.(a) 1st R. War. R. will capture 1st two objectives on the left in 2 waves, 1st wave to 1st objective, 2nd wave to 2nd objective

(b) H.B. will capture 1st two objectives on the right in 2 waves, 1st wave to 1st objective, 2nd wave to 2nd objective

(c) 1st Lon. S. I. will capture village of ROEUX in 2 waves, up to Black line.

(d) 1st R. Irish Fus. will capture 3rd objective on left in 2 waves

(e) 2nd Seaforth Hrs. will capture 3rd objective on the right in 2 waves.

1st R.W.R. N. Boundary, pencil line on map.
" S. " , dotted line from I19a89 - I20b5595
H.B. N. " , ditto
" S. " , dotted line E. corner of MT. PLEASANT WD - S. corner of Cemetery inclus. N. road thr. ROEUX to Black line - R. SCARPE from Black line to Blue line.

1st Lon. S. I. N. Boundary, ditto to Black line.
S. " , R. SCARPE

1st R. I. F. N. " , pencil line on map
S. " , from I19a89 - I20b85 - dotted line to I21b78

2nd Seaf. Hrs. N. " , ditto, DELBAR WOOD inclus.
S. " , E. Corner MT. PLEASANT WOOD - I20b03 - R. SCARPE.

6. Preliminary Moves.

1st R.M.R. leading wave will form up in front line, 2nd wave in new trench E. of CRETE.

H.B. leading wave as above, 2nd wave in N. of CEYLON.

1st R.I.F. leading wave in CRETE, 2nd wave behind embankment.

2nd Leic. Rs. ditto

1st Lon. I.T. leading wave in front line, 2nd wave in S. half of CEYLON.

7. The Attack

At zero hour there will be a creeping barrage in front of 1st R.M.R. + H.B., advancing at rate 100 yds. in 2 minutes.

At Zero –10 mins. leading wave of 1st R.M.R. + H.B. will move out of their trenches + lie down 20 yds. in front of their trench.

1st R.M.R. will advance on a 2 Coy: front in 2 waves, their 3rd Coy: following 1st wave closely as moppers up for CHATEAU + other buildings.

H.B. will advance on a 2 coy: front in 2 waves, with 2 platoons following 1st wave closely as moppers up for Cemetery + other buildings.

2 other platoons to follow closely + on leading wave reaching black line, these 2 platoons will form a defensive flank facing S. from I 20 b 03 – I 20 a 72.

Remaining Coy: of 1st R.W.R. & H.B. will be carrying Coy: & will remain behind embankment under orders of O.C. Battn.
1st Som. L.I. will attack on a 2 Coy: front, 3rd Coy: as moppers up, 4th Coy: carrying behind embankment.
1st R.I.F. will attack on a 2 Coy: front with 1 platoon in rear of 1st wave as moppers up, remaining 2 platoons of that Coy: forming a carrying party for 2nd Leaf. Hrs.
4th Coy: carrying party.
2nd Leaf. Hrs. on a 2 Coy: front, with 2 platoons 1st R.I.F. as carrying party under orders of O.C. 2nd Leaf. Hrs.

8. Artillery
At zero hour a heavy bombardment will be put down in ROEUX & continue till zero + 20 mins at which hour a heavy creeping barrage will advance thr. ROEUX at rate 100 yds in 4 mins. & at zero + 20 mins. 1st Som. L.I. will advance. see next page.

9. Time Table
Time table for advance on various objectives is attached as Appendix A.

10. Consolidation.
1st R.W.R. & H.B. will dig lunette trenches on

* 9 cont.

(b) Map showing timings of barrage lifts is attached. Copies will be issued later down to Platoon Comdrs.

(c) At the commencement of each advance a salvo of smoke will be fired from all guns. This signal will also be used in subsequent operations involving a new artillery programme.

(d) 4 inch Stokes Mortars will discharge Thermite from Zero to Zero +10 mins. on woods W. of ROEUX.

(e) Gas.

Gas will be discharged from LIVENS projectors after dark on Y day eg. against village of ROEUX, if wind is favourable.

arriving at Black line.
When Blue line is captured, consolidation will start at once & a strong line will be made by reversing parapet of CYPRUS Tr.
R.E. will make strong points in rear.
When Red line is captured, this will be consolidated at once, & strong patrols will be sent round S. edge of PLOUVAIN.

11. 10th M.G. Coy:
(a) 2 sections are placed under orders of Div.
Remaining 2 secs. will move from embankment behind 2nd waves of 1st R.W.R. & H.D. & take up a position on highest ground E. of GAVRELLE – ROEUX Rd.
O.C. 2 secs. under the Div. will report by wire to Bde. H.Q. when his work under the Div. is completed.

(b) 10th T.M. Batty.
2 guns will bombard Cemetery & 2 guns wood W. of ROEUX previous to Zero hour.
After Black line is captured they will move forward there & be prepared to move to Blue line directly that is captured, to bombard HAUSA & DELBAR WOODS in case of a counter attack.

12. Signal Communications.

A visual Stn. will be permanently manned near Bde. HQ. at H23d 48 by Bde. Sig. Sec. When Black line is captured, Bde. Sig. Sec. will establish another visual Stn. near CHEMICAL WORKS.

Adv. Report centre will move to Chalk Pit I 13d 55, where all messages will be sent & where there will be a relay of runners.

Bns. will establish forward visual Stns. to communicate with Bde. Sig. Stn. near CHEMICAL WORKS.

13. Moves of HQ.

Bde. HQ. will remain at H23 b 21

1st R.W.R. & H.B. HQ. will not move beyond Black line.

1st Lan. F. HQ. may move from embankment into ROEUX when that village & Black line is captured.

1st R.I.F. & 2nd Sea. Hrs. will establish their HQ. in embankment previous to zero hour & may move to Black line when Blue line is captured.

14. Equipment etc.

Every man will carry a pick or shovel in

proportion of 2 shovels to 1 pick.
All moppers up will carry P bombs & proportion of Mills grenades.
Every man will carry 2 Mills grenades & 2 sand bags.
Aeroplane flares will be distributed amongst all battns.

15. Z day will be May 3rd
Zero hour will be notified later.
An officer from each unit will report at Bde. H.Q. at 7 p.m. 2nd inst. to synchronise watches.

16. Acknowledge.

Issued at 12 noon.

K. G. C. Fellowes Capt
Brigade Major
10th Inf. Bde.

Appendix A.

Time Table of Advances.

	Pass present front line	Reach Black line	Leave Black line	Reach Blue line	Leave Blue line	Reach Red line
1st R.W.R. 1st wave	0	0+22	.	.	.	.
2nd wave			0+41	0+55	.	.
A.B. 1st wave	0	0+22	.	.	.	.
2nd wave			0+41	0+55	.	.
1st N.I.F[illegible] 1st wave					0+85	0+101
2nd wave					[illegible]	
2nd Leif.[illegible] 1st wave					0+85	0+101
2nd wave						
1st [illegible]	0+16					

"A" Form.

MESSAGES AND SIGNALS.

No. of Message

Prefix .... Code .... m. | Words | Charge

Office of Origin and Service Instructions.

Sent

At .... m.

To ....

By ....

This message is on a/c of:

.... *Service.*

(Signature of "Franking Officer.")

Recd. at .... m.

Date ....

From ....

By ....

TO

Ref BIACHE Sh. 1/20.000.

Sender's Number.	Day of Month.	In reply to Number.	AAA
*			

RESUME of 10th BDE. Operation Orders No. 28.

1. 4th Div will take part in a general attack to-morrow.

2. FRONTAGE FRESNES-LES-MONTAUBAN - PLOUVAIN.

3. VI Corps will attack S. of SCARPE.

4. 10th BDE will attack on the right with 1st SOMERSET L.I attached.
   12th BDE will attack on the left.

5. 10th BDE. Boundaries
   Northern X roads H 18 d 5510 - I 13 d 1.5 - thence straight line to I 16 a. 0.0.
   Southern - RIVER SCARPE (1st SOM. L.I).

6. Objectives 1. BLACK LINE } Vide
   2. BLUE " } Map
   3. RED "

7. Household Bn & 1st R. Warwicks will capture the first two objectives - 1st wave - 1st objective.
   2nd wave - 2nd objective.

From

Place

Time

The above may be forwarded as now corrected.

(Z)

Censor.

Signature of Addressor or person authorised to telegraph in his name.

* This line should be erased if not required.

750,000. W 2186 -M509. H. W. & V., Ld. 6/16.

"A" Form.

MESSAGES AND SIGNALS.

Army Form C.2121
(in pads of 100).
No. of Message

Prefix .... Code .... m.	Words	Charge	This message is on a/c of:	Recd. at .... m.
Office of Origin and Service Instructions.	Sent		.... Service.	Date
	At .... m.			From
	To			
	By		(Signature of "Franking Officer.")	By

TO (2).

Sender's Number.	Day of Month.	In reply to Number.	AAA
	2nd		

1st SOMERSET L.I will capture ROEUX in two waves up to BLACK LINE.
1st R. IRISH FUS. will capture 3RD objective on Left.
2nd SEAFORTH HIGHLRS " " " " " RIGHT, passing through Household Bn.
8. HOUSEHOLD BN. BOUNDARIES
N. I 19 a 8 9 – I 20 b 55 95.
S. Dotted line from E. Corner of MOUNT PLEASANT WOOD – S corner of CEMETERY (inclusive) – N. road through ROEUX to BLACK LINE – thence to RIVER SCARPE & onwards to BLUE LINE.
1st SOM. L.I on right in front line
1st R. WARWICKS " Left " " "
9. ZERO HOUR – 3.45 A.M.
10. BARRAGE at Zero hour (i) creeping barrage will commence advancing at rate of 100 yards

From in two minutes. (ii) Heavy bombardment will
Place be put on ROEUX & continue for 20 minutes –
Time then creep forward at 100 yards in 4 minutes.

The above may be forwarded as now corrected. (Z)

Censor. Signature of Addressor or person authorised to telegraph in his name.

* This line should be erased if not required.

750,000. W 2183–M509. H. W. & V., Ld. 6/16.

"A" Form.

MESSAGES AND SIGNALS.

Army Form C.2121 (in pads of 100).

No. of Message

Prefix ... Code ... m.	Words	Charge	This message is on a/c of:	Recd. at ... m.
Office of Origin and Service Instructions.	Sent		... Service.	Date
	At ... m.			From
	To			
	By		(Signature of "Franking Officer.")	By

TO (3)

Sender's Number.	Day of Month.	In reply to Number.	
*	2nd		AAA

At commencement of each advance a salvo of smoke will be fired from all guns: this signal will also be used in subsequent operations involving further artillery preparation.

Trench Mortar Battery will bombard CEMETERY previous to Zero hour & WOODS W. of ROEUX at Zero + 10 mins.

II. ~~At Zero ... H.B. & R. Warwicks will ... out of their trenches & lie down in front of them.~~

III. Advance. H.B. will advance on two Coy. front in two waves with two platoons following 1st wave closely as Moppers up for CEMETERY & other buildings. Two other platoons following closely as Moppers up will form a defensive flank from I 20 b 0.3 to I 20 d 7.2 – facing SOUTH – as soon as 1st wave have taken BLACK LINE.

From

Place

Time

The above may be forwarded as now corrected. (Z)

Censor. Signature of Addressor or person authorised to telegraph in his name.

* This line should be erased if not required.

750,000. W 2186–M509. H. W. & V., Ld. 6/16.

"A" Form.
MESSAGES AND SIGNALS.

Army Form C.2121
(in pads of 100).
No. of Message

Prefix .... Code .... m. | Words | Charge
Office of Origin and Service Instructions.
Sent
At .... m.
To ....
By ....
This message is on a/c of:
.... Service.
(Signature of "Franking Officer.")
Recd. at .... m.
Date ....
From ....
By ....

TO

(4)

Sender's Number.	Day of Month.	In reply to Number.	AAA
*	2nd		

Remaining Coy will be a carrying Coy
& will stay behind embankment under
orders of O.C. Battalion.
13. On reaching BLACK LINE, H.B. will
dig LUNETTE trenches.
14. On reaching BLUE LINE, H.B. will
consolidate at once & make strong line
by reversing parapet of CYPRUS trench.
15. R.E will make strong points in rear.
16. 10th M.G. Coy - two sections will move
behind 2nd waves of H.B. & 1st R. Warwicks
& will take up position on highest ground
E. of GAVRELLE-ROEUX road.
17. BDE. H.Q will remain at H23 b 2.1.
1st R WAR. H.Q. will not move beyond BLACK LINE
H.B. " " " " " " " "
1st Som. L.I " " may move from embankment to ROEUX.

From
Place
Time

The above may be forwarded as now corrected.
(Z)
Censor. Signature of Addressor or person authorised to telegraph in his name.
* This line should be erased if not required.
750,000. W 2186-M509. H. W. & V., Ld. 6/16.

"A" Form.
Army Form C.2121
(in pads of 100).

MESSAGES AND SIGNALS.

No. of Message

Prefix ... Code ... m. Office of Origin and Service Instructions.	Words	Charge	This message is on a/c of: ... Service. (Signature of "Franking Officer.")	Recd. at ... m. Date ... From ... By ...
	Sent At ... m. To ... By ...			

TO (5)

Sender's Number.	Day of Month.	In reply to Number.	AAA

18. Equipment Every man will carry a pick or shovel, two Mills bombs & two Sandbags.
Aeroplane flares will be distributed.
Moppers up will carry P bombs & proportion of Mills Grenades.
Ratio of picks & shovels – two shovels to one pick.
19 Signal communication. Visual station at BDE. H.Q.
After capture of BLACK LINE another will be established near CHEMICAL WORKS
Battns will establish visual stations to get into touch with BDE visual station.
Advanced report centre will move to CHALK PIT I 13 d 5 5.

From
Place
Time

The above may be forwarded as now corrected, (Z)
Censor. Signature of Addressor or person authorised to telegraph in his name.

* This line should be erased if not required.

750,000. W 2186 – M509. H. W. & V., Ld. 6/16.

MESSAGES AN[D SIGNALS]

... Code ... m.	Words	Charge	This message is on a/c of:	Recd. at ... m.
Office of Origin and Service Instructions.			... Service.	Date ...
	Sent			From ...
	At ... m.			
	To ...			
	By ...		(Signature of "Franking Officer.")	By ...

TO

Sender's Number.	Day of Month.	In reply to Number.	AAA
*			

	[illegible]	R.B	Leap	Reserve	L Blue	Reach
1st H.W	F.L	Line	B.L	Blue L	Line	Red Line
1st W	0	0+22				
2nd W			0+41	0+55		
H.B						
1st W	0	0+22				
2nd W			0+41	0+55		
[illegible]						
1st W					0+85	0+101
2nd W						
Seaforth [illegible]						
1st W					0+85	0+101
2nd W						
1st Bn [illegible]	0+16					

From

Place

Time

The above may be forwarded as now corrected.

(Z)

... *Censor.*

Signature of Addressor or person authorised to telegraph in his name.

* This line should be erased if not required.

750,000. W 2186–M509. H. W. & V., Ld. 6/16.

Household Battn.

Narrative of operations May 3rd – 4th 1917

The Household Battn. was detailed to seize the two objectives known respectively as the BLACK & BLUE lines – vide 10th Inf Bde O.O. No 28. The Royal Warwickshire Regt was to attack on the left with the same two objectives in view whilst the Somersetshire Light Infantry (attached to the 10th Inf Bde for operations) were to take & hold that portion of the BLACK line that lay between the right of the Household Battn & the SCARPE to the E of ROEUX village.

The Household Battn was ordered to attack on a two Coy frontage with two platoons in each wave – 1st wave to take 1st Objective – 2nd wave 2nd objective – ½ a company to act as moppers up for the buildings round CEMETERY & the remaining half to form a defensive flank facing South from I 20 b 0.3 to I 20 a 7 2. Braches sheet 1/20,000. until the Somerset Light Infantry who were to start 10 mins later, had taken their objective.

Following these instructions I issued my orders vide Battn. O.O. attached.

At 9-30 pm on May 2nd the Battn. moved into their position in the assembly trenches which had been cleared the whole of the day to allow the heavy artillery to bombard

the [illegible] round the CEMETRY and CHATEAU.
I visited the front line and support trenches and found all the men in position by 11-30 pm.
Battn HQrs was situated at the Embankment (named CRUMP later)
In order to try and keep in touch with the trend of events I sent Lieut Canalet as forward observing officer to a spot approximately I 19 c. 4.7 together with two signallers who establish a line with Battn HQrs
At Z hour 3-45 AM it was still very dark and the darkness – as I heard later – was increased by a heavy smoke barrage which caused the waves to begin to lose direction almost immediately.
No reliable information reached me for some considerable time, as my forward observation post was unable to report anything owing to the smoke and the darkness.
Information from two wounded N.C.Os however, pointed to one or two isolated parties having pushed forward across the ROEUX – GAVRELLE Rd whilst the greater number appeared to be held up in front of the CEMETERY and in front of the ROAD S of CORONA trench, owing to very heavy M.G fire.
The first authentic report came through the Somersetshire Light Infantry who were almost

owing to snipers and as this was not possible in the open, but a report came through from a Sergt of the Royal Warwickshire Regt at 11-7 AM to say that 40-50 of the Bde were holding out along the ROEUX-GAVRELLE Rd. – Later on we heard that most of these had been taken prisoner by the enemy. At ~~about~~ 12-30 pm I sent forward two bombing parties up CORONA trench under 2nd Lieut Waklyn to work forward as far as possible and then block the trench. This movement was ordered by Lt Col. Forster Royal Warwickshire Regt – commanding the front line system, & it was to ~~[illegible]~~ co-operate with some patrols of the Royal Irish Fusiliers and Royal Warwickshire Regt working up towards the CHATEAU. The bombing party worked forward along CORONA trench until the trench came to a dead end which was much blown in & here it established itself. The patrols that were working on its flanks having met with a good deal of opposition were unable to establish themselves as far advanced. Several small parties of the enemy were seen on the E side of the ROEUX-GAVRELLE road by my bombing parties and a MG was located & reported.

In the meantime the enemy counter-attacked near the CHEMICAL WORKS but our artillery dispersed them, tho' they were reported to have ~~taken~~ captured some of our [illegible]diately checked in their advance through ROEUX WOOD by intense M.G. fire.

In view of this the O.C. Seaforths and I after talking the matter over decided to telephone to the 10th Bde HQrs to ask for a Battn to come up in support in order to attack ROEUX village from the direction of MT PLEASANT WOOD & thus relieve the pressure in the WOOD itself. This message was sent at 5-10 AM, but ~~[illegible]~~ ~~[illegible]~~ this suggestion was not consented to.

Soon after this I had an order from the Bde to send out to my forward posts and tell them to consolidate where they were and also to send out two platoons from my carrying Coy to support the defensive flank on my right. I was on the point of
5 AM to 5-30 AM sending out runners with orders accordingly when information came through to say that most of my men were back again in the front line trenches. I sent up Lieut Cuyaler to clear up the situation and he returned about 6-15 telling me that this was the case and that only one officer – 2nd Lieut Barker had returned. I then ordered 2nd Lieut Wauklyn
6-38 AM with two platoons from my carrying Coy to go up & re-organize the front line and hold the same order as we had ~~[illegible]~~ assembled in. At 10-45 AM I received an order from the Bde to try and push forward scouts to see whether we were holding out near the CEMETERY

a[illegible]anced posts.

Enemy artillery had been fairly quiet after the counter-barrage had ceased – and for the remainder of the day the line remained inactive.

After dusk several small parties & individuals who had been lying in no-mans-land returned to the line, and it was ascertained that no one remained holding out in the neighbour-hood of the CEMETRY.

At 10 pm I received orders from Lt Col Forster to establish a line of posts from I 19.c.6.6 to W edge of CEMETRY. Work was to have commenced at 11 pm but owing to the difficulty of getting my working parties organised, & as my orders did not reach the front line until 11 pm 10-30 pm, work was not commenced until after 12 midnight. My orders were to dig a line of 9 posts at about 50 yards interval and to man them when they were complete. Owing to the fact however, that the ground had not been properly reconnoitred by daylight with a view to digging the posts & that they were started somewhat hurriedly the officer in charge took a wrong direction and the posts were established in a more easterly direction than they should have been. On the following night however I had this rectified & the line as laid down was established and held.

The above completes the operations from 2 a.m. May 3rd until dawn on May 4th. During this time we suffered the following casualties:–

Officers
Killed – 4
Missing – 3
Wounded – 3
total 10

O R
Killed – 16
Wounded – 91
Missing – 114
221 total

Practically all of which were caused by M.G. fire.

On May 6th at the suggestion of the G.O.C. 10th Inf. Bde I attempted to organise a local attempt against the enemy trench line in ROEUX WOOD. A patrol was sent out under 2nd Lieut Moffat to reconnoitre the position and altho' the information brought in was valuable & gave accurate siting of hostile M.G.s etc I did not think it wise to attempt a raid in the limited time that remained before daylight. I contented myself by sending 3 small parties to bomb the enemy listening posts. This small offensive caused the enemy considerable alarm & an intense barrage was the result. Several of our bombs

7

w[illegible] reported to have reached their objectives. Our casualties ~~were~~ only amounted to one man slightly wounded in the shoulder.

15/5/17

[illegible]
Major
[illegible] Battn.

"A" Form.

Army Form C.2121
(in pads of 100).

MESSAGES AND SIGNALS.

No. of Message

Prefix ....Code ....m. | Words | Charge | This message is on a/c of: ....Service. (Signature of "Franking Officer.") | Recd. at ....m. Date .... From .... By ....

Office of Origin and Service Instructions.

Sent At ....m. To .... By ....

TO

Sender's Number. | Day of Month. | In reply to Number. | AAA

*

A.B. Supplementary Operation Orders.

1. Platoons will make their objectives as follows –

No. I from road at I.19.b.3.0 to road I.19.b.6.2

No. II from road I.19.b.6.2 – angle of BLACK LINE I.19.b.7.3

No. III. From I.19.b.7.3. to straight line running through N.E. corner of CEMETERY & cutting BLACK LINE at I.19.b.6.4.

No. IV I.19.b.6.4 to BDE. boundary at I.19.b.5.6

2. (a) Care must be taken to establish communication with 1st E. LANCASHIRE Regt. (11th INF. BDE.) on LEFT & R.I.F. on right as soon as possible AAA Should either flank be left open a defensive flank must be

From

Place

Time

The above may be forwarded as now corrected. (Z)

Censor. Signature of Addressor or person authorised to telegraph in his name.

* This line should be erased if not required.

750,000. W 2186–M509. H. W. & V., Ld. 6/16.

"A" Form.

MESSAGES AND SIGNALS.

Army Form C.2121 (in pads of 100).

No. of Message

Prefix ... Code ... m.	Words	Charge	This message is on a/c of:	Recd. at ... m.
Office of Origin and Service Instructions.	Sent		... Service.	Date
	At ... m.			From
	To			
	By		(Signature of "Franking Officer.")	By

TO

Sender's Number.	Day of Month.	In reply to Number.	AAA
*			

formed & consolidated as quickly as possible
(b) Boundary mark between H.B. & R.I.F. will be marked by a telegraph post on ROEUX Road S. of X roads.
3 2nd Seaforth Highlanders - Moppers up.
Dispositions
· 1 group + 2 L.G.s in trench W. of ROEUX - GAVRELLE road.
4 groups of moppers up round X Roads.
2 " " " on the left.
1 " " " on extreme right.
When their work is completed they will return to trench W. of ROEUX & remain in local support.
4. M.G.s - 2 M.G. sections (2 guns per section) will come on in rear of the Seaforths together with one section of 9th Field Coy - R.E.

From
Place
Time

The above may be forwarded as now corrected. (Z)

Censor. Signature of Addressor or person authorised to telegraph in his name.

* This line should be erased if not required.

750,000. W 2185–M509. H. W. & V., Ld. 6/15.

"A" Form.

Army Form C.2121
(in pads of 100).

MESSAGES AND SIGNALS.

No. of Message

Prefix ... Code ... m.	Words	Charge	This message is on a/c of:	Recd. at ... m.
Office of Origin and Service Instructions.	Sent		... Service.	Date
	At ... m.			From
	To			
	By		(Signature of "Franking Officer.")	By

TO (3)

Sender's Number.	Day of Month.	In reply to Number.	AAA
*	15th		

4 (continued) M.G.s will come right through the Seaforths & establish themselves in the front line in the neighbourhood of X roads - CEMETERY & work in co-operation of the Household Bn. AAA One section will watch roads S. of X roads leading to ROEUX - the other will watch the left flank. An Officer will be i/c of each section

5. Should support be required it should be notified through Bttn. H.Q. which will MOVE to near junction of CORDITE & CEYLON before Zero hour. This should only be sent if absolutely necessary

6/ S.O.S. signals must only be sent up at danger points & not promiscuously

From

Place

Time

The above may be forwarded as now corrected. (Z)

Censor. Signature of Addressor or person authorised to telegraph in his name.

* This line should be erased if not required.

750,000. W 2186–M509. H. W. & V., Ld. 6/16.

MESSAGES AND [torn]

Prefix .... Code .... m. | Words | Charge | This message [torn]

Office of Origin and Service Instructions.

Sent

At .... m.

To ....

By ....

.... Service.

(Signature of "Franking Officer.")

From ....

By ....

TO (2)

Sender's Number.	Day of Month.	In reply to Number.	AAA
*	10		

along the line.

7. Bayonets must be fixed whilst doubling up to barrage to avoid showing up in the trenches before Zero hour.

8. 1 Section of 9th Coy R.E. will be sent up to help H.B. in wiring at night

9. Overhead M.G. fire will be maintained upon road running N.E. through ROEUX village.

Signed - John AM KIRKWOOD
Major.
Commanding Household Battn

From

Place

Time

The above may be forwarded as now corrected. (Z)

.... Censor. Signature of Addressor or person authorised to telegraph in his name.

* This line should be erased if not required.

750,000. W 2186—M502. H. W. & V., Ld. 6/16.

(1)

SECRET. Preliminary Instr. No: 1.

10th Bde. ~~O. O. No. 1 ..~~

9th May 1917

Ref. Map attached T.S. 2, 1/10,000

1. XVII Corps will resume the offensive with the object of gaining line ROEUX CEMETERY – CORONA – CUPID northwards. The attack will be carried out in 2 phases, on Z & Z+1 day.

2. (a) On Z day, 4th Div. will attack Black line see map attached. 17th Div. will assist 4th Div. on the North.

(b) On Z+1 day, 4th Div. will attack Blue line.

3. Boundaries.

(a) 10th Inf. Bde. will attack on the right,
11th " " " " " " left, on Z day.

(b) 11th Inf. Bde. " " Blue line on Z+1 day.

(c) Boundaries are shown on attached map. Household Bn. will attack on the left, with the Cemetery as Objective. 2nd Seaforth Hrs. will follow close in rear as moppers up for the buildings.

1st R. Irish Rer. will form a defensive flank on the right.
1st R. M. R. will be in support in present front line.

4. Preliminary Moves.
(a) On Z day the troops will be formed up in assembly areas before 4 a.m. & will remain there till Zero hour.
Household Bn. in front line as far as S. end of Mt. Pleasant Wood.
2nd Suffolk Rer. in CEYLON Tr., N. of June. with COLNE Tr.
1st R. I. F. in front line from S. end of Mt. Pleasant Wood.
1st R. M. R. in CRETE, & S. portion of CEYLON if necessary.
10th M. G. Coy: 1 section in front line with H. B.
1 " " " " " 1st R. I. F.
2 " under Div. Orders.
10th T. M. Batty. in front line under orders of 1st R. I. F.
(b) During the period from daylight to Zero hour, it is of paramount importance that the presence of troops should not be discovered by the enemy.
Special attention must be paid to concealment

from aerial observation & from enemy observers S. of the River.
Slits must be cut in the assembly trenches for latrines.
Ladders will be provided for the front line but these must be supplemented by making steps in the parapet.

5. Plan of Attack.

(a) At zero hour H.B. & 1st R. Irish Fus. with 2nd Seaforth Hrs. in close support to H.B. as moppers up for the Cemetery & buildings, will advance behind an intense creeping barrage, moving at rate 50 yds. in 2 minutes.

(b) H.B. will attack in one wave going straight through to their objective on the E. side of the buildings & will dig in at once.

(c) 2nd Sea. Hrs. will follow close up to the H.B. & will mop up the buildings & any trenches there, special parties being told off for definite localities.
This mopping up is to be considered of the very highest importance.

(d) 1st R. Irish Fus. will advance & dig in at once making certain they are in connection with H.B.

(e) 1st R. Lan. R. will move up at once into the front line via CEYLON, COX & COLNE Tr. & hold the front line.

(f) 1 sec. 10th M.G. Coy: will advance in rear of 2nd Leinf. Rts. & will at once take up positions to bring flanking fire in direction due N. & S.E.

(Reserve) 1 sec. 10th M.G. Coy: will advance ~~with~~ in rear of 1st R.I.F. to bring flanking fire to bear in the direction N.E. & South.

1 gun will be sent to S. post of 1st R.I.F. about I.19.c.5.1.

(g) 10th T.M. Batty. without guns will be under orders of 1st R.I.F. to dig in & form part of the garrison of the line.

(h) 2 days rations are being sent up on Y night, so that not more than 10 men per Bn. will be left near Bn. H.Q. as carrying party for S.A.A. & grenades.

(i) An adv. dump of S.A.A. & grenades will be formed in Sap at I.19.a.6.1.

6. Assembly Areas.

Every available man must be employed from today onwards in deepening front line especially near Mt. Pleasant Wood.

1st R.I.F. will continue work on COLNE Tr. with 10th T.L. Batty.

1st R.W.R. will concentrate on COX Tr.

7. Aeroplanes.

Special arrangements are being made to police the assembly areas by aeroplanes.

Bns. will establish Lewis Guns to fire against hostile aircraft.

O.C. 10th M.G. Coy: will detail 2 guns also for this purpose.

8. Prisoners.

A.P.M. will take over prisoners on the Athies – Fampoux Rd. near the German 4th Fy. stn, where prisoners should be sent in batches.

9. Zero dates & hours will be notified later.

10. Acknowledge.

[illegible] Capt.
Brigade Major
10th Bde.

Issued at 1 p.m.

Household Battalion.

Narrative of Operations, May 11th/12th.

BIACHE Sheet 1/20,000.

In accordance with Brigade Preliminary Instruction dated May 9th 1917

I issued the Battalion O.O. attached.

At 5.30p.m. on Z day I moved my Battalion H.Q. up to the head of CEYLON trench near the Junction with CAP. Here I established a telephone line in connection with the Brigade Report Centre. I also took Lieut.Cazalet forward as Intelligence Officer leaving Lieut.Dill with the greater part of the H.Q. staff at Battn H.Q. in CRUMP dug-outs.

At 6p.m. I went round the line and found the whole situation satisfactory - Officers and men keen and confident. Captains Tobin commanding the whole line, which was divided into 4 platoons, total 5 officers and 177 O.R.

At Z hour (7.30p.m.) I was able to obtain an excellent view of the commencement of the attack and the men went forward in very good order - scarcely one seemed out of place - Though I consider that in places the barrage was falling rather short and this caused my left platoon No.1 to bear away to the left after they had worked up close to the barrage - otherwise I saw no fault in the line up to the time that I lost them to view in the smoke.

At Z plus 5 I saw several prisoners come running back through the smoke towards Mt.PLEASANT WOOD.

At 8.15p.m. Capt.Tobin came by wounded, but informed me that all was going well.

At least 50 prisoners had passed my H.Q. by 8.15p.m.

A message brought in at 8.45p.m. stated that my left platoon (No.4) as well as part of No.3, had gained its objective and was consolidating.

At 8.50p.m. Lieut.McPherson of the Seaforths, who had been forward to clear up the situation (he did very valuable work during the night) returned to report that my left was alright, but that my right centre and right were held up in the gardens round the Cemetery and were being enfiladed by M.G.fire from the houses - he also informed me that there appeared to be a wide gap on again from there to the R.Irish Fusiliers. The Seaforth mopping up party had mostly returned to the trench which ran W. of the Cemetery across our front - this they were consolidating.

9p.m. I sent Lieut.Cazalet down at once to R.Warwickshire H.Q. to inform Colonel Forster, and asking him if I might use his front line Coy's to strengthen the position and gain ~~for~~ our objective.

I had been told that I should not use the troops holding our front line excepting in the case of a counter-attack and then only if very urgently needed.

Consequently I did not feel justified in using them unless I received the consent of the O.C. R.Warwickshire R. and the Brigade.

9.21p.m. At 9.21p.m. I received a reply back that I was to send forward "B" Coy R.War.R. and that one Company of the King's Own were coming up to reinforce the front line. (this amounted to less than 30) I then directed O.C."B"Coy. R.War.R. to advance at once, and support my right and right centre in the direction of the Cemetery. This order was send off in writing at

9.33p.m. 9.33p.m. I sent a runner off at the same time to 2nd Lieut. Stockwood who was the only officer ~~who was the only officer~~ whom I could ascertain to be in the advance line, telling him that support was being sent up to his right.

9.57p.m. A further message from O.C. R.War.R. arrived at 9.57p.m. saying that his "C" Coy was being sent up to establish communication between my left and the Hampshire Regt who were co-operating on the left of the 10th Brigade . Immediately on receipt of this I sent off a message in reply to say that all reports gave me to understand that we were linked up on the left and that my right was far more in need of support. This message

10.2p.m. I sent off at 10.2p.m. but in the meantime "C" Coy R.War.R. had already been despatched (I might here add that this rather pointed to overlapping, as I had been previously given to understand that all 3 Coys of R.War.R. were under my orders, and I was relying upon this in order to be able to deal with any urgent call for support - more especially as each Coy of R.War.R. was less than a full platoon strength.)

9.50p.m. At 9.50p.m. I heard from my right centre platoon that they had pushed forward and got in touch with the two left platoons, but had been entirely cut off from the right platoon. I gathered that the combination of the darkness and fairly heavy machine gun fire from houses in the neighbourhood of the cemetery had accounted for this.

10.38p.m. At 10.38p.m. I sent a message to O.C. SKEW, which message I repeated to the Brigade Major on the telephone(This was of very little use to me as the line was frequently broken during the night) to say that I was confident of holding the objectives gained and of consolidating the entire position providing that supports were sent to me to operate after moonrise or before dawn as the darkness rendered any attempt to straighten things out futile.

About this time I heard that part of "B" Coy. R.War.R. had run into machine gun fire and got separated, 14 of them had returned to the front line and the remainder (as I learnt later) had joined their "C" Coy and had consolidated on our left in touch with the Hampshire Regt, altho' I should have preferred their assistance on my right.

11.55p.m. At 11.55p.m. I received a message from O.C. R.War.R. telling me that if I utilized his remaining men, that he would send the Coy of King's Own up to occupy our front line in place of them.

12.35a.m. At 12.35a.m. I heard from Lieut.McPherson that three of the machine guns that were to have been with my advanced troops, if they took the objective were back with the Seaforths and that only one was up in my front line on the N.S. of the Cemetery.

1.5a.m. At 1.5a.m. I heard through a runner from 11th Brigade that all their objectives had been taken.

About this time the Brigade Major 10th Brigade arrived at my H.Q. and I told him that I felt confident about holding the position providing I could obtain enough men to send forward before dawn to capture the houses on the road round the Cemetery and I asked him to let me have at least 50 men of the King's Own as well as the remaineder of the R.War.R. This he agreed to do.

I then sent a further message to Lieut. Stockwood to hold on and to consolidate as energetically as possible.

There was some delay before the O.C. "A" Coy, R.War.R. and King's Own Coy arrived; in the meantime I sent a message to O.C. 10th Brigade M.G. in the Seaforth trenches, which I append.

2.45a.m. At 2.45 the Officers commanding detachments of R.War.R. and King's Own arrived, and I gave them the appended orders - This left 50 men of the King's Own to hold the front line and trenches in support.

4.30a.m. At 4.30a.m. I received a message through the Seaforths that both their parties had reached the houses round the Cemetery and X Roads and were clearing them.

4.54a.m. At 4.54a.m. everything appeared quiet in the houses from what I saw personally and I sent a message through to the O.C. King's Own advanced posts to establish communication with my right beyond the Cemetery.

5a.m. At 5a.m. I went up to the line held by my men and found all their posts had been consolidated and that they had established connection with the R.War.R's on their left and the King's Own on their right - but it appeared to me that the houses in rear of our line, S. of the Cemetery were still held by the enemy as I noticed flares being sent up from that direction in response to two enemy aeroplanes that were flying low over our line and firing very lights. I told Lieut. Stockwood to send two bombing parties to clear up some of the buildings directly he was able to find the available men. About 5.30a.m. as I was returning to CEYLON trench via CORONA, I met the Brigade Major, 10th Brigade and told him that the situation was satisfactory, excepting the clearance of the houses in question, and pointed out that we had not enough men to clear up the situation. He suggested that the Seaforths should send a strong detachment forward as bombing parties and I agreed that it was the best possible solution. Capt. Booth of the Seaforths was then instructed to go forward to clear the vicinity of the Cemetery at the same time as the 11th Brigade attacked the BLUE Line, viz 6.30a.m.

This was most effectively done and some 5 Officers and 60 O.R. were taken prisoners.

After this, everything quietened down, and the line was strengthened and consolidated.

During this engagement the enemy barrage was more prolonged than during the operations of May 3rd/4th, and continued several hours.

Casualties during the action -

<u>Officers</u>.

Killed	-	1.
Missing.	-	2.
Wounded	-	1.
		Total 4.

<u>O.R.</u>

Killed	-	3 and 1 Died of Wounds.
Wounded	-	68.
Missing	-	22 (includes 1 wounded).

16/5/17.

Sd/J.H.M.Kirkwood, Major,
Household Battn.

Confidential

War Diary
of
Household Battalion
from
1st June 1917
to
30th June 1917

Volume 8

W. Portal

Lieut Colonel
Commanding
Household Battalion

2/7/17

8/48

HOUSEHOL D BATTALION

List o f awards

No. 14 Tpr. (A /Cpl.of H.) Buckingham awarded Military Medal for:-

" On 11th. M ay when Battalion reached the objective he was the senior N.C.O. surviving.

While the men were digging in, he walked up and down the line under heavy machine gun fire from the village of ROEUX, which had not been cleared.

He showed the men the correct position in which they were to dig in and by his steadiness and fine example was mainly responsible for the success of the consolidation. This N.C.O. took part in the operations of the 11th. April and the 3rd. May as well as the 11th. of May and througho ut has shown himself a fine commander of men an d invaluable to the Battalion.

2/Lieut. J.Moff att. awarded the Military Cross for

" For the very praiseworthy and gallant manner in which he carried outa difficult and risky reconnaissance in ROEUX WOOD on th e night 6/7th. inst. He worked his way through the woo d and along the German front line , being several tim es subjected to heavy M.G. fire.

He located fiv e enemy machine guns and exactposition of supposed tank gun which information proved of great value in the successful operat ions of the 11st. inst. During the operatio ns of the past month this Officer has shown a fine ex ample of endurance and coolness, in action."

HOUSEHOLD BATTALION

LIST OF AWARDS

No. 832 Tpr. (A /Cpl.) Page awarded Military Medal for

" This N. C.O. was attached as Signalling N.C.O. to assaulting Coys. on 11th. May. Under very heavy shell fire of maching guns he laid a wire from the original front line to the advanced position.

The line was constantly broken and for 24 hours he was continually out mending regardless of maching gun fire and snipers. His perseverance was of the greatest assistance in getting information through quickly without risking the lives of runners.

In the operations of the 11th. April and 3rd. May he showed a fine example of gallantry and steadiness and his conduct throughout has been worthy of the highest praise."

Captain J.F.M .Sloan awarded Military Cross for

" This Officer established a dressing station in the centre of FAMPOUX on 11th. April where he dressed the wounded under very heavy shell fire, his dressing station being blown in on the top; he dressed over 200 cases under very difficult conditions having twice to change his dressing station and I cannot speak too highly of his conduct during those two days.

Instructions regarding War Diaries and Intelligence Summaries are contained in F. S. Regs., Part II. and the Staff Manual respectively. Title pages will be prepared in manuscript.

WAR DIARY
or
INTELLIGENCE SUMMARY.
(Erase heading not required.)

Army Form C. 2118.

Place	Date	Hour	Summary of Events and Information	Remarks and references to Appendices
HOUVIN. HOUVIGNEUL	June 1st 1917.		Batt^n Training. P.m. Div. Horse Show. Batt^n won one (2nd) Two (3rd) one (4th)	
	June 2nd		Batt^n Training	
	June 3rd		Church Parade. Draft 4 officers Lt P.C. Potter 2Lt H.J. Renaway 2Lt C. Clerk... 2Lt A.C. Barnard - & 111 O.R. arrived	
	June 4th		Scheme at LIGNEREUIL. Specialists. Batt^n Strength 685 O.R. Off 23.	
	June 5th		Batt^n Training - Scheme on reconnaissance for Junior officers & N.C.Os at LIGNEREUIL in afternoon.	
	June 6th		Batt^n Training. Weather exceedingly hot this month	
	June 7th		Inter platoon Competition. Forced March. Assault Course. 15 rounds the field. No 13 Platoon won. No 16 ... second.	
	June 8th		Scheme for Consolidation around LIGNEREUIL.	
	June 9th		Route March	
	June 10th		Presentation of Medal Parade by Gen Lambton. Capt Sloan received the Military Cross. C.Q.M.S. Buckingham & Page received the Military Medal.	
	June 11th		Heavy rain - Batt^n prepared to move	
ARRAS	12/6/17.		Battalion moved from HOUVIN-HOUVIGNEUL to ARRAS by bus. Battalion billeted in Deaf & Dumb School Rue des Augustines. Lt ROGERS & 270 O.R detached for duty with 184th Tunnelling Coy.	
	13/6/17		Company Training near St CATHERINES.	R...

Instructions regarding War Diaries and Intelligence Summaries are contained in F. S. Regs., Part II. and the Staff Manual respectively. Title pages will be prepared in manuscript.

WAR DIARY
or
INTELLIGENCE SUMMARY.
(Erase heading not required.)

Army Form C. 2118.

Place	Date	Hour	Summary of Events and Information	Remarks and references to Appendices
ARRAS	14/6/17		Company training at St CATHERINES. Party of 200 found to carry Lievens projectors up to the front line at night. Party of 80 for wiring GAVRELLE Switch.	
	15th		Company training. Major J. H. M. KIRKWOOD awarded D. S. O., Lt MOFFAT & 2nd Lieut BARKER awarded the Military Cross. Lt J. H. C. SIMPSON 4th Div. R.F.A attached pending transfer.	
BALMORAL CAMP G 18 a 2.8. Refsh ARRAS 1/10.000.	16th		Battalion moved by route march to BALMORAL CAMP - G 18 a 2.8. Only a few dug outs & shelters existed on arrival, but camp was pitched with bell tents & tarpaulins. Parties of 120 found for wiring.	
	17th		Camp improved & wired in. Shelters built & accomodation enlarged. A working party of 200 under Lieut Moffat from Nos 2 & 3 Coys was found to carry LIEVENS projectors to the line.	
Refsh. Plouvain 1/10000	18th		At about 12.15 a.m 2nd Lieut J. E. LOWRIE, i/c of the leading party of No. 3 Coy carrying the projectors, was killed by a shell just north of ROEUX village: he was buried at H 24 d 7.8. Parties of 220 found for wiring intermediate line, Gavrelle Switch, carrying mine-shaft frames & for work on the PELVES ROAD.	Ref [illegible] Capt [illegible]

T2134. Wt. W708—776. 500000. 4/15. Sir J. C. & S.

Instructions regarding War Diaries and Intelligence Summaries are contained in F. S. Regs., Part II. and the Staff Manual respectively. Title pages will be prepared in manuscript.

WAR DIARY
or
INTELLIGENCE SUMMARY.
(Erase heading not required.)

Army Form C. 2118. 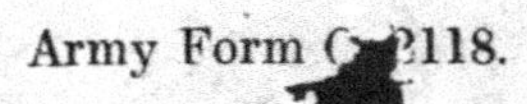

Place	Date	Hour	Summary of Events and Information	Remarks and references to Appendices
BALMORAL CAMP.	19th		10th BDE relieved 12th Bde in left sector of the line. 2nd Seaforth Highlrs on left sub-sector, 1st R. Warwickshire Regt on right sub-sector. 1st R Irish Fusiliers in support, Household Battalion in reserve. 100 men working on Blue line.	
	20th		Company training. Working party of 200 found at night. 100 men under Lt Cazalet reporting to 2nd Seaforth Highlrs, + 100 under Capt Tealon reporting to 1st R Warwickshire Regt in the line.	
	21st		Company training. Hut erected in camp for Headquarter mess. Work on drainage continued.	
	22nd		Battalion relieved 2nd Seaforth Highlrs in left sub-sector from I 8 c 3.1 - I 14 a 50.25 (to COCOA trench exclusive). For dispositions + map vide Append I.	Append. I.
	23rd		Relief complete at 2.20 A.M. Lateness caused by enemy barrage put down on front + support lines in reply to friendly barrage further north. Communication established with 9th Bn (Duke of Wellington's) West Riding Regt on our left (52nd Bde 17th Division) + 1st R. IRISH FUS. on our right. 'C' Coy of 3/4th (Queen's) R. West Surrey Regt attached in sections for instructional purposes - vide Appendix II	[illegible] Append. II.

T2134. Wt. W708–776. 500000. 4/15. Sir J. C. & S.

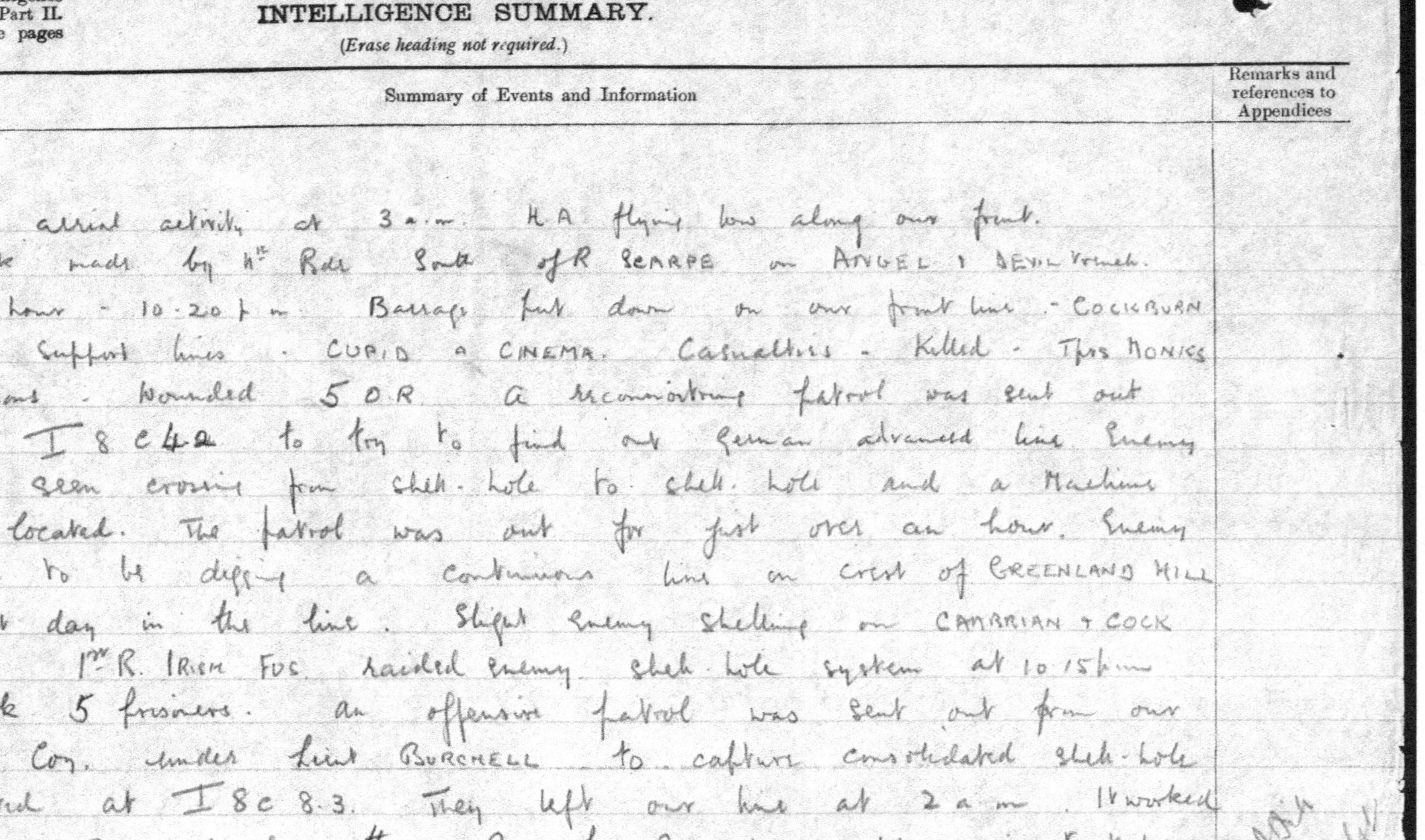

Instructions regarding War Diaries and Intelligence Summaries are contained in F. S. Regs., Part II. and the Staff Manual respectively. Title pages will be prepared in manuscript.

WAR DIARY
or
INTELLIGENCE SUMMARY.
(Erase heading not required.)

Army Form C. 2118.

Place	Date	Hour	Summary of Events and Information	Remarks and references to Appendices
Front line. left sub-sector.	23rd		Enemy aerial activity at 3 a.m. H A flying low along our front. attack made by 4th Div South of R SCARPE on ANGEL & DEVIL trench. Zero hour - 10.20 p.m. Barrage put down on our front line - COCKBURN and support lines. CUPID & CINEMA. Casualties - Killed - Ptes MONIES & Parsons - Wounded 5 O.R. A reconnoitring patrol was sent out from I 8 c 4 2 to try to find out German advanced line. Enemy were seen crossing from shell-hole to shell-hole and a Machine Gun located. The patrol was out for just over an hour. Enemy found to be digging a continuous line on crest of GREENLAND HILL	
	24th		Quiet day in the line. Slight enemy shelling on CAMBRIAN & COCK C.T.s. 1st R. Irish Fus. raided enemy shell hole system at 10.15 p.m & took 5 prisoners.	
	25th		An offensive patrol was sent out from our left Coy. under Lieut BURCHELL to capture consolidated shell-hole located at I 8 c 8.3. They left our line at 2 a.m. It worked E for 200 yards then S. for 30 yds & W again to take post in rear. It was found unoccupied but a telephone wire	[illegible]

T2134. Wt. W708—776. 500000. 4/15. Sir J. C. & S.

Instructions regarding War Diaries and Intelligence Summaries are contained in F. S. Regs., Part II. and the Staff Manual respectively. Title pages will be prepared in manuscript.

WAR DIARY
or
INTELLIGENCE SUMMARY.
(*Erase heading not required.*)

Army Form C. 2118.

Place	Date	Hour	Summary of Events and Information	Remarks and references to Appendices
Front line left sub-sector.	25th		was found & four German water-bottles were left in a dug-out in the post. A patrol went out from our right Coy. & reconnoitred the N bank of railway cutting. It was out for an hour & heard enemy's working parties. They were fired on by snipers & forced to return. Pte. SQUIBB - No 3 Coy runner was killed on Railway at 1 a.m. Wounded 7 O.R.	
			Enemy shelled COCKBURN & CINEMA at 9.15 a.m for half an hour. Trenches blown in here & there but little damage was caused	
			At night patrols were sent out to reconnoitre line of German shell-holes which were found to be unoccupied.	
			During night of 24/25th & day of 25th No. 1 Coy relieved No 2 Coy in left front line, No. 4 Coy relieved No 3 Coy in right front line. No 2 Coy going into reserve & No 3 to support.	
	26th		Quiet in the front line. At 9.45 a.m a 5.9 shell dropped in CRUSH trench wounding Major MOOREHOUSE of 12th Manchester Regt & 5 of No 2 Coy.	
			Battalion relieved by 12th Battn Manchester Regt, 52nd Bde, 17th Div.	[illegible]

A5834 Wt. W4973/M687 750,000 8/16 D. D. & L. Ltd. Forms/C.2118/13.

Instructions regarding War Diaries and Intelligence Summaries are contained in F. S. Regs., Part II. and the Staff Manual respectively. Title pages will be prepared in manuscript.

WAR DIARY
or
INTELLIGENCE SUMMARY.
(Erase heading not required.)

Army Form C. 2118.

Place	Date	Hour	Summary of Events and Information	Remarks and references to Appendices
Front line left sub-sector	26th		2nd Seaforth Highlrs took over line just north of R SCARPE. Brigade thus being on one Battalion frontage	
STIRLING CAMP H13d75	27th		Relief complete 1.50 A.M without casualties. Battalion marched to Bde Reserve at STIRLING CAMP (H13 d 7.5.) Battalion all in camp by 4.40 A.M. Total casualties in the line - O.R. 3 killed 22 wounded.	
Ref Sh. 51b N.W. 1/20.000)	28th		Company training in ROCLINCOURT VALLEY G 9 b & G 10 a. Working party for digging out CUSP trench in support line found - 3 officers & 100 O.R left camp at 8.45 P.M.	
	29th		No's 1 3 & 4 Coys training. No. 2 Company started to make rifle range & final assault course at H 7 c 5.2. Draft of 1 officer (2nd Lieut C.H. DAVIES) and 121 O.R. arrived at 11.50 p m from 4th Div. Depot Battalion SAVY.	
	30th		No's 2 3 & 4 Coys training. No 1 Coy working on rifle range. 1st R. Warwickshire Regt relieved 2nd Seaforth Highlrs in the line.	

R[illegible] Capt. & Adjt.

T2134. Wt. W[illegible]776. 500000. 4/15. Sir J. C. & S.

APPENDIX I

Dispositions of HOUSEHOLD BATTN in left sub-sector of 10TH BDE frontage from night of June 22nd/23rd to night of 26th/27th.

Front line

Right Company – 1 platoon in COAL trench and posts. Lewis Gun on each side of railway cutting
1 platoon in COCKBURN with three sections S of Railway in CROFT up to junction with COCOA exclusive.
L.G in COCKBURN.
1 platoon + Coy. H.Q. in CUPID.
1 platoon 3/4th QUEENS in COCKBURN.

Left Company
1 platoon + two L.Gs in COCKBURN to junction with CAMBRIAN (inclusive)
2 platoons + Coy. H.Q with 1 L.G in CUPID. 1 L.G in CURLY
1 platoon of 3/4th Queen's in COCKBURN + COD.

Support Coy
3 platoons in CINEMA.
1 " " QUARRY.
1 platoon 3/4th QUEENS in CUBA.

Reserve Coy in CRUSH trench with an A.A. L.G post by day at H 18 d 8.5.
1 platoon 3/4th QUEENS attached.

Rations for front line + Support Coys were taken in limbers to QUARRY + carried up to line by reserve Coy – for Reserve Coy + Battn H.Q were brought direct to Bn. H.Q.

Water was obtained from FAMPOUX LOCK + carried up in petrol tins by Reserve Coy.

SKETCH to accompany APPENDIX I

H.I.

1,2 · 7 · 8 · 18 · 13 · 14

GREENLAND HILL
COST
WINDMILL
TO PLOUVAIN →
COD
CURLY
CUBA
CAMBRIAN
CROOK
CROW
CINEMA
CUPID
COCKBURN
COAL
CROFT
COCOA
CHEMICAL
COUNT
CAMEL
← TO FAMPOUX
QUARRY
STATION
CHEMICAL WORKS
CRUSH
L.G. POST.
BATTN H.Q.
CHATEAU
TO ROEUX ↓
R. SCARPE

MAGNETIC

British trenches.
German trenches.
British posts.
German posts.
Railway.
Battalion Boundary

SCALE
1/10.000

APPENDIX II.

"C" Coy 3/4th (Queens) R. WEST SURREY Regt were attached to the Battalion while in the line. They were first in sections attached to platoons, but on the 28rd were formed into platoons & attached to Coys as shown in Dispositions (Appendix I).

Extract from Report on the Coy sent into Brigade by Lieut Col W. R. PORTAL

... "With referance to their work while they were with us, both officers & men were very keen & gained much practical experience during those four days.

They had fairly heavy casualties (28 O.R. 1 officer) but their moral did not suffer in consequence.

The points in which they require more practice are –

1. Control of men in trenches by N.C.O's & Section leaders.
2. Sanitation
3. Working while in the line.
4. Care of arms & equipment."

Ru[illegible] Capt & Adjt.

4th Division

War Diaries

10th Infantry Bde

Household Battn.

~~July – December~~

~~1914~~

1917 JULY 1 – 1918 FEB

DISBANDED

CONFIDENTIAL.

WAR DIARY

of

HOUSEHOLD BATTALION

from

1st July 1917

to

31st July 1917.

Volume. 9

Lieut-Colonel.
Commanding
Household Battalion.

3rd August 1917.

Instructions regarding War Diaries and Intelligence Summaries are contained in F. S. Regs., Part II. and the Staff Manual respectively. Title pages will be prepared in manuscript.

WAR DIARY
or
INTELLIGENCE SUMMARY.
(Erase heading not required.)

Army Form C. 2118.

Place	Date	Hour	Summary of Events and Information	Remarks and references to Appendices
STIRLING CAMP. H13d7.5. Refsh. 51b N.W 1/20.000	1st July.		Company training. Party of 30 O.R under 2nd Lieut. E.N. de GEIJER detached for duty with N.Z Tunneling Coy. "PIRBRIGHT" rifle range completed. Working party of 3 officers & 100 O.R found for work on front line at night.	
	2nd		Company training. Working party of 3 offrs + 100 O.R as above.	
	3rd		"	
	4th		" " Letter of approbation received from Major General Hon. W LAMBTON C.V.O. C.B. C.M.G. D.S.O. on condition of Transport. Battalion marched from STIRLING CAMP at 6 p.m & relieved 2nd SEAFORTH HIGHLANDERS in Brigade Support in Railway Cutting H23 a & c (less one Coy.) No 4 Coy. relieved one Coy of 2nd Seaforths in CRUMP Trench (H24d) & came under the orders of 1st R. IRISH FUSILIERS who relieved 1st R WARWICKSHIRE Regt & became front line Battalion.	
	5th		Party of one officer & 30 O.R. attd to N.Z Tunneling Coy attached to Durham Field Coy R.E at Railway Triangle H19 central. Following working parties found - By day 2 officers & 80 O.R working	R. J. Bull Capt & Adjt

T2134. Wt. W708—776. 500000. 4/15. Sir J. C. & S.

Instructions regarding War Diaries and Intelligence Summaries are contained in F. S. Regs., Part II. and the Staff Manual respectively. Title pages will be prepared in manuscript.

WAR DIARY
or
INTELLIGENCE SUMMARY.
(Erase heading not required.)

Army Form C. 2118.

Place	Date	Hour	Summary of Events and Information	Remarks and references to Appendices
Railway Cutting H23 a 4 e	5th		in two shifts on dug-out accomodation in Railway Cutting. By night - 1 officer + 18 O.R. wiring CORONA trench. 3 offrs + 100 O.R. working on CEYLON + CABBAGE trenches	
	6th		Same parties found by day + night as above. C. of H. HAMILL went out on patrol on this night to reconnoitre N. bank of R. SCARPE E of ROEUX Bridge with a view to crossing place for future operations. This patrol be repeated each night from 6th - 13th inclusive.	
	7th		Same parties by day + night as above. C. of H. HAMILL located three enemy posts on S. bank of R. SCARPE.	
	8th		Same parties by day + night. 3 men killed on party at night - vide	Appendix 'B'
	9th		" " " " . Lt. GILBEY, 2nd Lts. WILLIAMSON + BYGOTT joined the Battn.	
	10th		Battalion relieved 1st R. IRISH FUSILIERS in Brigade sector. No. 4 Coy on the right (Capt. C.A.F. TEULON), No. 3 Coy on the left (Lt. J. MOFFAT). No. 1 Coy in Support (Lt. V.A. CAZALET), No. 2 Coy in Reserve (Lt. T.H.C. SIMPSON).	
	11th		Relief complete 12.55 a.m. 2nd Lieut. BURCHELL took out	R... Capt. ...

T2134. Wt. W708-776. 500000. 4/15. Sir J. C. & S.

Instructions regarding War Diaries and Intelligence Summaries are contained in F. S. Regs., Part II. and the Staff Manual respectively. Title pages will be prepared in manuscript.

WAR DIARY
or
INTELLIGENCE SUMMARY.
(Erase heading not required.)

Army Form C. 2118.

Place	Date	Hour	Summary of Events and Information	Remarks and references to Appendices
10th Brigade Sector - Lines before ROEUX.	11th		and established three posts 50 yards in advance of our line of 1 N.C.O & 3 men each. For disposition see Appendix "A". 2nd Lieut DAVIES & C of H HAMILL patrolled N. bank of R. SCARPE locating enemy posts on S. bank as before. Artillery normal during the day	Appendix "A"
			Patrols were sent out under 2nd Lt. BURCHELL, Cpl GAWTREY, & 2nd Lt DAVIES. Enemy wire located & reconnoitred by two former & N. bank reconnoitred by 2nd Lt DAVIES & C of H HAMILL.	
			Barrage put down by our artillery S of the river from 10.50 - 11 p.m. Enemy trench mortars active.	
			Posts established last night advanced fifty yards & a fourth added. Now on line I 20 a 7 5 - I 20 a 7.9.	
			Lettered A B C D. 2nd Lieut GIBBS was responsible for the re-establishment of these.	
	12th		Enemy T.M.s active at morning stand-to. Day quiet. Patrol sent out from right Coy. reconnoitred enemy wire & post on R. bank opposite our No 1 Post. (Cpl ANSETT & 2 men)	R. [illegible]

Instructions regarding War Diaries and Intelligence Summaries are contained in F. S. Regs., Part II. and the Staff Manual respectively. Title pages will be prepared in manuscript.

WAR DIARY
or
INTELLIGENCE SUMMARY.
(Erase heading not required.)

Army Form C. 2118.

Place	Date	Hour	Summary of Events and Information	Remarks and references to Appendices
Lines before ROEUX.	13th		12.30 AM – 12.33 a.m. Thermite bombardment of enemy shell-hole system carried out by "O" & "Q" sections of No 4 Special Coy. R.E. with 4 Stokes mortars. A box barrage put round bombarded area by artillery. At zero plus 4 (12.34 a.m) Lt. BURCHELL took out a fighting patrol of 8 men with a Lewis Gun from junction of CROFT & COLOMBO, C of H. RAYNER with 6 men going out from No 3 Post. Both patrols worked E for over 200 yards but enemy seemed to have vacated the area temporarily as no signs of living, or recently dead, men were found. Patrols returned at 2 a.m. Enemy retaliation for bombardment very slight. A B C & D posts withdrawn at 12 midnight & re-established 12.35 a.m. Day quiet. Patrol under C.of.H. RAYNOR sent out at night to investigate enemy shell holes located by him on previous night. Found unoccupied. Coy. relief carried out. No 2 Coy relieved No. 4, No. 1 Coy	R. J. Dill Capt & Adjt
	14th		relieved No. 3. Parties of 40 from No. 1 Coy & 80 from No 3 Coy.	

T2134. Wt. W708—776. 500000. 4/15. Sir J. C. & S.

Instructions regarding War Diaries and Intelligence Summaries are contained in F. S. Regs., Part II. and the Staff Manual respectively. Title pages will be prepared in manuscript.

WAR DIARY
or
INTELLIGENCE SUMMARY.
(Erase heading not required.)

Army Form C. 2118.

Place	Date	Hour	Summary of Events and Information	Remarks and references to Appendices
	14		dug a communication trench from COLOMBO to D post & a fire trench joining "A" post to COLOMBO salient. 2nd Lieut GIBBS was entirely responsible for the laying out of this work. On his way back after relief a gas-shell killed his runner, Spr. DOWNIE & gassed him slightly – vide Appendix "B"	Appendix "B"
			Searching barrage put down by our artillery on enemy sector in front of us, from 2 a.m. – 2.50 a.m.	
			Day quiet. Patrol under Cpl. WILKINSON leaving our No. 1 post at 11 p.m. penetrated enemy post on N. bank of river & brought back full report & useful information. Shell hole found unoccupied.	
			Work was continued on linking up posts. "A" to COLOMBO was completed, "D" to COLOMBO dug down to 5 feet. D to C begun & "A" to B dug down 2 feet 6". Work interrupted by enemy machine gun fire & snipers who were very active.	
	15th		Enemy T.M.s very active at stand to. Artillery retaliation obtained. 125th & 128th Btys R.F.A. shot on German post at I20 d 20.85	R.W.F. Dill Capt & Adjt

T2134. Wt. W708—776. 500000. 4/15. Sir J. C. & S.

Instructions regarding War Diaries and Intelligence Summaries are contained in F. S. Regs., Part II. and the Staff Manual respectively. Title pages will be prepared in manuscript.

WAR DIARY
or
INTELLIGENCE SUMMARY.
(Erase heading not required.)

Army Form C. 2118.

Place	Date	Hour	Summary of Events and Information	Remarks and references to Appendices
Lines before ROEUX	15		at 4 pm & 6 pm. Two Germans were killed & one ran away. This was in preparation for scheme to cross the river at night & attack German dug-out located by Lt Davies & C. of H. HAMILL at I 20 c 5.5. At 11.50 pm party of 10-12 of the enemy tried to cut the wire in front of our No 1 post. They were observed & L.G. & rifle fire opened. They advanced & bombed the post but were driven off with L.G. & bombs. Two dead were left. Our casualties - 2nd Lt WHITELAW slightly wounded. Major KIRKWOOD D.S.O. left the Battn to command 9th Duke of Wellington's (17th Divn).	APPENDIX B.
	15/16.		At 12 midnight 2nd Lt C.H. Davies, C of H. HAMILL & four men swam the river at I 20 c 5.6. They were observed by Germans on S bank. 6 of the enemy ran down from an E direction & opened heavy fire on them from 15 yds range. They reached the S. bank & found it wired. When they got disentangled Lt Davies saw that it was hopeless trying to proceed so ordered the men to return. They dived & swam back covered by party	R. W. Dill Capt & Adjt

T2134. Wt. W708-776. 500000. 4/15. Sir J. C. & S.

"A" Form. Army Form C. 2121

MESSAGES AND SIGNALS. No. of Message ....

Prefix .... Code .... m.	Words	Charge	This message is on a/c of:	Recd. at .... m.
Office of Origin and Service Instructions.	Sent		.... Service.	Date ....
SECRET	At .... m.			From ....
	To			
	By		(Signature of "Franking Officer.")	By ....

TO APPENDIX "A".

Sender's Number.	Day of Month.	In reply to Number.	AAA
* RD 218	13th		

Dispositions of Battalion in Brigade Sector.

Right Coy.

	No 1 Post	–	1 NCO + 10 men with Lewis Gun
	No 2 Post	–	1 N.C.O + 9 men
	No 3	–	2 NCO + 16 " with Lewis' Gun
	No 4	–	1 NCO + 6 men
	No 5	–	2 NCO + 10 "
	No 6	–	1 N.C.O + 6 "
	No 7	–	1 NCO + 6 men with Lewis Gun & Snipers post

Local Support in CORONA 2 N.C.O + 20 men

The posts are divided into three sectors each having an officer & Senior N.C.O

From

Place

Time

The above may be forwarded as now corrected. (Z)

Censor. Signature of Addressor or person authorised to telegraph in his name.

* This line should be erased if not required.

225,000. W 14042–M 44. H. W. & V., Ld. 12/15.

"A" Form.
Army Form C. 2121

MESSAGES AND SIGNALS.

No. of Message ....

Prefix .... Code .... m.	Words	Charge	This message is on a/c of:	Recd. at .... m
Office of Origin and Service Instructions.	Sent		.... Service.	Date ....
	At .... m.			From ....
	To			
	By		(Signature of "Franking Officer.")	By ....

TO (2)

Sender's Number.	Day of Month.	In reply to Number.	AAA
* RD218	13		

in charge.

No 1 Sector. Nos 1, 2 & 7 posts
Senior N.C.O in No 2 Post by day
Officer in advanced H.Q.

No 2 Sector – Nos 3 & 4 Posts
Senior N C O in No 3 by day
Officer at advanced H.Q.
Advanced H Q just in rear of
No 3 Post –
2 offrs + 7 O R
(2 Sgts 4 S Bs 1 sen. N.C.O.)

No. 3 Sector Nos 5 & 6 posts
Local Support (with Senior N.C.O.)
Officer in Coy H.Q.

Coy H Q in ROEUX WOOD
Coy Commander & officer i/c of No 3 sector
+ 15 O.R.

From
Place
Time

The above may be forwarded as now corrected. (Z)

Censor. Signature of Addressor or person authorised to telegraph in his name.

* This line should be erased if not required.

225,000. W 14042 M 44. H. W. & V., Ld. 12/15.

MESSAGES AND [SIGNA]LS. No. of [Message]

Prefix .... Code .... m. | Words | Charge
Office of Origin and Service Instructions.

Sent
At .... m.
To ....
By ....

This message is on a/c of:
.... Service.
(Signature of "Franking Officer.")

Recd. at .... m
Date ....
From ....
By ....

TO (3)

Sender's Number.	Day of Month.	In reply to Number.	AAA
* RD218	13th		

Listening Posts (by night)
1/ 1 NCO & 2 men between No. 1 & 2 Posts
2/ 1 NCO + 4 men with Lewis Gun 30 yards E of No. 3 Post
Lewis Gun kept in dug-out at No. 3 Post by day
Total Strength of Coy –
4 officers and 120 OR

Left Company – 3 platoons
No 1 Platoon – In COLOMBO from junction of CROFT – COLOMBO to junction of CEYLON – COLOMBO (exclusive) 1 Lewis Gun at each end. Total Strength 1 officer & 37 O.R.

From
Place
Time

The above may be forwarded as now corrected. (Z)
Censor. Signature of Addressor or person authorised to telegraph in his name.

* This line should be erased if not required.

225,000. W 14042–M 44. H. W. & V., Ld. 12/15.

Army Form C. 2121.
(In pads of 100.)

MESSAGES AND SIGNALS.

No. of Message..........

Prefix..........Code..........m	Words.	Charge.	This message is on a/c of:	Recd. at..........m.
Office of Origin and Service Instructions.	Sent		..........Service.	Date..........
	At..........m.			From..........
	To..........			
	By..........		(Signature of "Franking Officer.")	By..........

TO (4)

Sender's Number.	Day of Month.	In reply to Number.	AAA
*	14.		

No 2 Platoon

1 section with Lewis Gun in CROFT

1 section with Lewis Gun in COLOMBO support

2 sections in CABBAGE

1 officer + 4 platoon H.Q at junction of CROFT & CABBAGE.

Total strength 1 off 36 O.R.

No 3 platoon 1 N.C.O + 3 men in A post

" B "

" C "

" D "

2 sections + platoon H Q in CORONA near Coy H.Q

Officer lives at Coy H.Q.

A B C + D posts relieved every

From

Place

Time

The above may be forwarded as now corrected. (Z)

Censor. Signature of Addressor or person authorised to telegraph in his name.

* This line should be erased if not required.

(3198.) Wt. W 12952/M1294. 375,000 Pads. 1/17. H. W. & V., Ld. (E. 818.)

"A" Form.

MESSAGES AND SIGNALS. No. of Message..........

Prefix.......... Code.......... m	Words.	Charge.	This message is on a/c of:	Recd. at .... m.
Office of Origin and Service Instructions.	Sent		.... Service.	Date
	At........m.			From
	To			
	By		(Signature of "Franking Officer.")	By

TO (5)

Sender's Number.	Day of Month.	In reply to Number.	AAA
*	14		

24 hours. Total 1 offr 36 O.R.
Coy H.Q in CORONA -
Coy commander + 14 O.R
Total Strength of Coy
4 officers 123 O.R.
Support Coy in CRETE with 1 platoon
in CRUMP. Strength 2 officers
& 124 O.R.
Reserve Coy in CRUMP.
Strength. 3 officers & 148 O.R.
Battn H.Q in CRETE
Strength 1 offrs 38 O.R.
Regimental Aid Post in CRUMP
Total Strength
17 officers 518 O.R.

From
Place
Time

Rushbell
~~Capt. Adjt~~
for O C 8 CUD

The above may be forwarded as now corrected. (Z)

Censor. Signature of Addressor or person authorised to telegraph in his name.

* This line should be erased if not required.

(3198.) Wt. W 12952/M1294. 375,000 Pads. 1/17. H. W. & V., Ld. (E. 818.)

Instructions regarding War Diaries and Intelligence Summaries are contained in F. S. Regs., Part II. and the Staff Manual respectively. Title pages will be prepared in manuscript.

WAR DIARY
or
INTELLIGENCE SUMMARY.
(Erase heading not required.)

Army Form C. 2118.

Place	Date	Hour	Summary of Events and Information	Remarks and references to Appendices
Lines before ROEUX.	16.		on N. bank. They got back with only one slight casualty - Pte. BROWN (2619) wounded in the neck. The party of Germans on the S bank had been rifle-grenading our No. 1 Post in co-operation with hostile attack. 2nd Lieut. B. ROCHFORD joined the Battalion.	
	16/17		Battalion relieved at night by 2nd SEAFORTH HIGHLRS.	
	17		Relief complete 12.45 a.m. Battn marched to STIRLING CAMP to Brigade Reserve.	
	18.		Draft of 76 awaiting us at Stirling Camp were absorbed into the Coys. 2nd Lieut A.G BARNARD + 30 O.R. relieved 2nd Lt E.N de GEIJER on work with Durham Field Coy R.E.	
	19.		Company training. Party of 3 officers + 100 O.R. found for work in the line at night (No. 2 Coy.)	
	20.		Company training. 2nd Lieuts. GIBBS, KENNAWAY + WHITELAW rejoined from hospital. Letter of appreciation received from B.G.C. on work done by No 2 Coy in the line last night. Carrying party of 1 officer + 50 found at night.	R. J. Bell Capt + adjt

T2134. Wt. W708—776. 500000. 4/15. Sir J. C. & S.

Instructions regarding War Diaries and Intelligence Summaries are contained in F. S. Regs., Part II. and the Staff Manual respectively. Title pages will be prepared in manuscript.

WAR DIARY
or
INTELLIGENCE SUMMARY.
(Erase heading not required.)

Army Form C. 2118.

Place	Date	Hour	Summary of Events and Information	Remarks and references to Appendices
STIRLING CAMP	21st		Company training. Party of 3 officers 100 O.R. (No 4 Coy) found for work in the line at night. Capt Sloane M.O. returned from leave.	
	22nd		Divine Service. Major General Lambton attended. Nos 2 & 3 coys fired on range at Butte de Tir (G 20 a)	
	23rd		Company training. 2/Lt H.J. Kennaway left for "Rest Camp".	
	24th		Battalion Parade. 3 Officers 100 O.R. (No 2 Company) found for work in the line at night.	
	25th		Company training. Party of 3 officers 100 O.R. (No 1 coy) went for work in the line at night	
	26th		Company training. 3 officers 100 O.R. found from No 3 coy for work in the line at night.	
	27th		Company training. Preparation for relief on night of 28th.	
	28th		Battalion relieved Warwicks. Relief completed by 12.6 am. Patrols went out	
	29th		Quiet day except for Minnenwerfer. Corp of Horse Hamill awarded bar to military medal.	
	30th		During morning enemy shelled our area. Wiring and digging done at night	
	31st		Company relief. Relief completed by 12.30 am.	J. P. T. Burchell 2/Lt for Capt & Adj

T2134. Wt. W708—776. 500000. 4/15. Sir J. C. & S.

APPENDIX B

CASUALTIES from night 4/5th July 1917 to night 16/17th July 1917.

No	Rank and Name	Casualty	Date	Remarks.
731	Tpr. Dickenson. F.	Killed	8-7-17.	
2292	Tpr. Heath. F.J.	Killed.	8-7-17.	
141	Tpr. McElmurray.G.	Killed.	8.7-17.	
	2/Lt. P.N.Gibbs.	Wounded(Gas)	14.7.17.	Rejoined 19.7.17
2546	Tpr. Holyoake. R.C.	Killed.	14.7.17.	
2490	Tpr. Birch. H.	Killed.	14.7.17.	
2231	Tpr. Downie. F.	D of W.	14.7.17.	
2530	Tpr. Booker.H.	Wounded.	12.7.17.	
1558	L/Cpl. Hogg. J.	Wounded.	12.7.17.	D of Wds. 13.7.17
523	Tpr. Street. O.	Wounded.	14.7.17.	
1545	Tpr. McLachlin. G.	Killed.	15.7.17.	
2504	Tpr. Wigman.	Wounded.	15.7.17.	
	2/Lt. G.L. Whitelaw.	Wounded.	16.7.17.	Rejoined 19.7.17
2619	Tpr. Brown. W.	Wounded.	16.7.17.	
1175	Tpr. Hart. S.	Wounded.	16.7.17.	
2525	Tpr. Turner. J.	Wounded.	16.7.17.	
1719	A/C of H. Rumney.	Wounded.	13.7.17.	D of Wds. 14.7.17.

Vol 10

Household Battalion

War Diary

Volume 10

R W G Dill Captain & adjutant
for Lieut. Colonel
Commanding
Household Battalion

3.9.17.

Instructions regarding War Diaries and Intelligence Summaries are contained in F. S. Regs., Part II. and the Staff Manual respectively. Title pages will be prepared in manuscript.

WAR DIARY
or
INTELLIGENCE SUMMARY.
(Erase heading not required.)

Army Form C. 2118.

Place	Date	Hour	Summary of Events and Information	Remarks and references to Appendices
			troublesome all day	~~APP 8~~
	31st		Enemy quiet. Intercompany relief. Nos 1 – 3 companies relieved Nos 2 – 4 coys relief completed by 12·30 am.	~~APP 9~~
	Aug 1st		Everything exceptionally quiet during the day but at night enemy Minnenwerfer were peculiarly active.	~~APP 10~~
	2nd		Enemy artillery and minnenwerfer very quiet. Defence scheme for Battalion in Line was practised during the early part of the night. Wiring and digging in front line was carried on with.	~~APP 11~~
	3rd		Enemy activity nil. 2nd Seaforth Highlanders relieved us to-night and we were made Battalion in support, occupying the "cutting" H23 a&c. The relief was completed by 11.45 pm, No 2 company was left in CRUMP Trench till the night of 7th–8th	~~APP 12~~
	4th		Supplied working parties in Cutting and at night for the line.	~~APP 13~~
	5th		Working parties supplied.	~~APP 14~~
	6th		Working parties supplied. The raiding party 50 from No 2 and 50 from No 1 with 3 officers went to Blue Line	~~APP 15~~
	7th		3/10th Middlesex relieved the Household Battalion at 2·30 pm. No 2 company in CRUMP trench was not relieved till 9·30 pm. The Bn became reserve at STIRLING CAMP	APP 16

[signature] Burchell 2/Lt. a. Adjt

T2134. Wt. W708–776. 500000. 4/15. Sir J. C. & S.

Instructions regarding War Diaries and Intelligence Summaries are contained in F. S. Regs., Part II. and the Staff Manual respectively. Title pages will be prepared in manuscript.

WAR DIARY
or
INTELLIGENCE SUMMARY.
(*Erase heading not required.*)

Army Form C. 2118.

Place	Date	Hour	Summary of Events and Information	Remarks and references to Appendices
CUTTING H25 a & c and STIRLING CAMP H15 d 5.5.	8th		No 2 company arrived in STIRLING CAMP H15 d 5.5 at 1.0 am There was a kit inspection by Capt Laughton in the morning. The new draft of 113 O.R with 2/Lt BUTLER who had joined the details on the previous day joined their respective companies. 2/Lt BUTLER being appointed to No 2 Coy.	
	9th		Company training. Fatigue company went to fill up shell holes to form ground. Lt SCOTT arrived and posted to No. 2.]	
	10th		Company training. Party of 1 offr. 70 O.R went to dig Cable trench at night	APP 16
	11th		Company training as usual. Party of 1 offr. and 75 O.R went to dig cable trench at night 9.15 pm	APP 17
	12th		At 5 am 1 N.C.O and 12 men went to report to New Zealand Tunnelling Co. to dig in Cutting. Church parade on parade ground at 9.30 am. Working party by night for digging Cable Trench at Bde ADQRS at 9.15 pm consisting of 1 offr. and 75 O.R.	APP 18
	13th		Company route marches. Aquatic sports in the afternoon at which Gen Laughton attended and distributed the prizes. Working party of 1 officer and 75 O.R by night to dig cable trench. Party of 100 men employed during day on improvement of camp	APP 19
	14th		Company training and Baths. At night 1 officer and 75 O.R went to dig cable trench at 9.15 pm. at Bde (advance) Headquarters. 100 O.R. used during day improving camp	APP 20
	15th		Company training. Camp has been greatly improved by duckboarding and draining.	J. R. [illegible] 2/Lt APP 21

T2134. Wt. W708—776. 500000. 4/15. Sir J. C. & S.

Instructions regarding War Diaries and Intelligence Summaries are contained in F. S. Regs., Part II. and the Staff Manual respectively. Title pages will be prepared in manuscript.

WAR DIARY
or
INTELLIGENCE SUMMARY.
(*Erase heading not required.*)

Army Form C. 2118.

Place	Date	Hour	Summary of Events and Information	Remarks and references to Appendices
STIRLING CAMP	16th		Company training. During the day 100 men were employed for the improvement of the camp. 1 officer and 75 O.R. were detailed to work at Bde Headquarters advanced to dig cable trench at 9.15 pm.	[illegible]
	17th		Company training. The usual party of 100 men was employed in digging foundations for new sheds in camp.	[illegible]
	18th		The morning spent in striking camp. At 9.0 pm we went up to the front line and relieved 3/10th Middlesex. Relief was complete by 11.40 pm. Nos 4 & 3 Companies held front line, whilst 2 & 1 were in support in CRUMP. No 4 Coy held the right subsector of left Brigade front, No 3 held left. Three patrols were sent out during the night. One went and observed by gap in German wire. The other went out from No 1 post for 100 yards along the river bank but heard and saw nil. The third patrol acted as listening post.	
CRETE TRch				[illegible]
	19th		The day was quiet. At night we sent out three patrols as during previous evening. The party along river bank ran up against some 20 Boche and was forced to retire, two of our men were wounded and one missing, believed killed. Enemy trench mortars active during night.	[illegible]

J. R. J. [illegible] 2/Lt A/Adj

T2134. Wt. W708—776. 500000. 4/15. Sir J. C. & S.

Army Form C. 2118.

Instructions regarding War Diaries and Intelligence Summaries are contained in F. S. Regs., Part II. and the Staff Manual respectively. Title pages will be prepared in manuscript.

WAR DIARY
or
INTELLIGENCE SUMMARY.
(Erase heading not required.)

Place	Date	Hour	Summary of Events and Information	Remarks and references to Appendices
CRETE TR	20th		During the day enemy front line fired on by 18 pdr batteries. Enemy trench mortars very active during night. One patrol went out from D post and lay by gap in enemy wire. The enemy could be heard working and talking. Wire was put out	~~APP 26~~
	21st		All quiet during the day, at night enemy trench mortars. Patrols went out and did no particular work of value. Wiring was carried out.	~~APP 27~~
	22nd		The day was quiet as usual; but at night enemy trench mortars were bad.	~~APP 28~~
	23rd		During the day artillery put harassing fire on German front line system. Patrols went out at night and found nothing of exceptional value to report. The patrols all lay stress on the fact that the German wire is very thick. We increased our barbed wire defences. At night we were troubled with trench mortars.	~~APP 29~~
	24th		As usual the day proved quiet. At night the enemy attempted to raid D and No 2 post but they were driven off by Lewis gun and rifle fire. Trench mortars were again very active.	~~APP 30~~
	25th		The artillery put over some 150 rounds into German front line during the afternoon. This proved efficacious, especially as the night was quiet. Wiring was got on with.	~~APP 31~~

T P J Burchall [?]
2/Lt. [?]
A/Adjt

T2134. Wt. W708—776. 500000. 4/15. Sir J. C. & S.

Instructions regarding War Diaries and Intelligence Summaries are contained in F. S. Regs., Part II. and the Staff Manual respectively. Title pages will be prepared in manuscript.

WAR DIARY
or
INTELLIGENCE SUMMARY.
(Erase heading not required.)

Army Form C. 2118.

Place	Date	Hour	Summary of Events and Information	Remarks and references to Appendices
CRETE TR	26th		To-day the Battalion was relieved by the 3/10 Middlesex; the relief was complete by 12.30 am. The weather being so bad delayed relief by 2 hours. The battalion returned as reserve battalion to STIRLING CAMP	~~App 32~~
STIRLING CAMP	27th		The morning was occupied in inspecting equipment. A fellow was accidentally shot in a shelter by his comrade whilst the latter was cleaning his rifle.	~~App 33~~
	28th		A Brigade scheme for training brought out and companies start to carry it out	~~App 34~~
	29th		Company training. Fatigues used to improve condition of the Camp.	~~App 35~~
	30th		Company training. Received intimation that the Division will leave this area very shortly. A demonstration of the yukon pack given by Mackenzie of the Seaforth Hghs.	~~App 36~~
	31st		Company training south of the river in preparation to scheme laid down in Bde scheme. Baths at Candle Factory for whole day.	~~App 37~~

J. B. T. Burchell
2/Lt
A/Adj.

Confidential

War Diary

— of —

Household Battalion

— from —

6th November 1916

— to —

30th November 1916

Volumn No. 1.

Kilmorey
Major
for Lieut. Colonel
Commanding
Household Battalion

1.12.16

Vol I

CONFIDENTIAL

Vol XI

HOUSEHOLD BATTALION

WAR DIARY

VOLUME 11

From September 1st. to September 30th.1917

3.10.17.

Lieut.Colonel
Commanding
The Household Battalion.

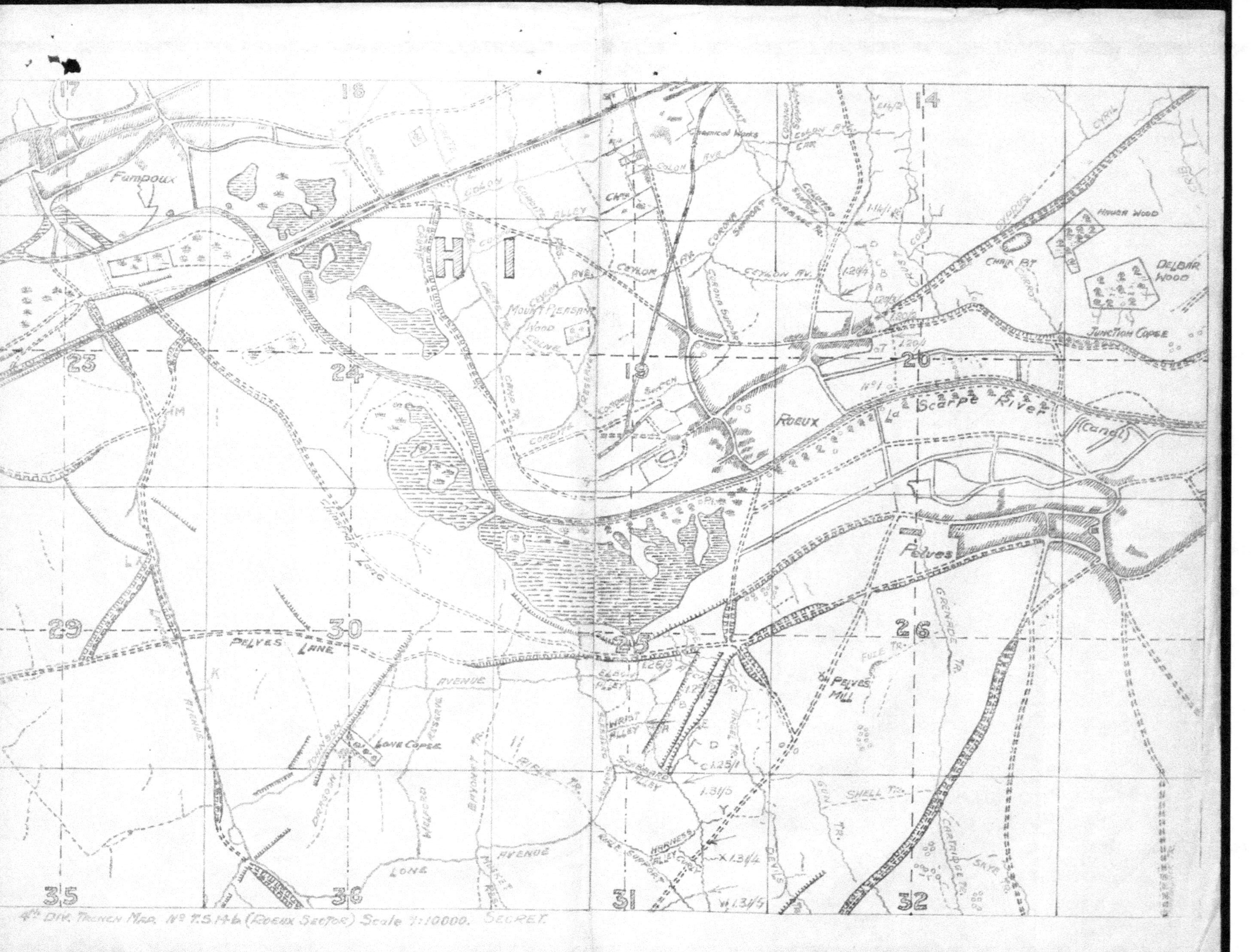

4th DIV. TRENCH MAP. No T.S.14.b (ROEUX SECTOR) Scale 1:10000. SECRET.

Instructions regarding War Diaries and Intelligence Summaries are contained in F. S. Regs., Part II. and the Staff Manual respectively. Title pages will be prepared in manuscript.

WAR DIARY
or
INTELLIGENCE SUMMARY.
(Erase heading not required.)

Army Form C. 2118.

Place	Date	Hour	Summary of Events and Information	Remarks and references to Appendices
STIRLING CAMP	1st		To-day we celebrated the anniversary of the formation of the battalion. We had a small ceremonial parade and march past to the Colonel on the foot-ball ground at [illegible] CAMP. Later on during the morning a funeral service was held over the body of Capt. Pember [illegible] Batt. which had recently been found near Roeux [illegible]. Capt. Pember had been killed on 3rd May. The funeral took place at the cemetery near Transport. In the afternoon there were inter company sports for the men.	
	2nd		Brigade tactical scheme was carried out near [illegible] during 8 am till 4 pm. Battalion practiced attack on three objectives on two Coy. frontages.	
CRETE TR.	3rd		The Battalion went into the line and relieved 2nd/[illegible] Middlesex and became front line battalion. Patrols were sent out at night. Enemy's wire was found to consist of 6 rows in parts.	
	4th		Patrols were sent out to break enemy sap. Sap was unoccupied. Enemy trench mortars below normal.	
	5th		The enemy put over 200 trench mortar gas shells during early morning. No casualties.	
			J. R. T. Burchell 2/Lt.	

T2134. Wt. W708—776. 500000. 4/15. Sir J. C. & S.

Army Form C. 2118.

Instructions regarding War Diaries and Intelligence Summaries are contained in F. S. Regs., Part II. and the Staff Manual respectively. Title pages will be prepared in manuscript.

WAR DIARY
or
INTELLIGENCE SUMMARY.
(*Erase heading not required.*)

Place	Date	Hour	Summary of Events and Information	Remarks and references to Appendices
CRETE TR	6th		The Battalion was relieved tonight by 6th Cameron Highlanders. The battalion went to Arras by train and were billeted for the night at Levis Barracks	
ARRAS.	7th		The Battalion proceeded by march to Bailleulval where we are to rest for about a fortnight.	
	8th		Refitting and baths.	
	9th		The Assaulting troops were rebilleted and are to train separately from details, and are to live separately.	
	10th		Company training as per Brigade training programme.	
	11th		Company training on the various training areas. A [illegible] pack competition for preliminary Brigade competition:- won by No 3 Coy.	
	12th		Usual training with inspection of gas respirators and helmets.	
	13th		Field firing scheme; specialist classes in the afternoon.	
	14th		Divine Service up on ground alongside transport lines.	
	15th		Company training	
	16th		Company training. Lecture on Carrier pigeons by R.E. officer Lt Harking.	
	17th		Companies partook in Battalion scheme.	
	18th		Ceremonial parade, and inspection by Brig-Gen Pritchard.	

J. G. [illegible] Burdett 2/Lt.

Instructions regarding War Diaries and Intelligence Summaries are contained in F. S. Regs., Part II. and the Staff Manual respectively. Title pages will be prepared in manuscript.

WAR DIARY
or
INTELLIGENCE SUMMARY.
(Erase heading not required.)

Army Form C. 2118.

Place	Date	Hour	Summary of Events and Information	Remarks and references to Appendices
Bailleulval.	19th		No 2 coy proceeded at 6.0 am to PROVEN Stn to work under instructions of R.T.O	
PROVEN.			The battalion paraded 10.0 am and proceeded to SAULTET L'ARBRET where it entrained and started at 2.2 pm for PROVEN. Arrived at PROVEN 2.0 am.	
	20th		Rest.	
	21st		Commanding Officers parade at 8.30 am, and subsequently a 12 kilometres route march. We are now in 5th Army and 14th Corps instead of 3rd Army 17th Corps	
	22nd		Company training	
	23rd		Divine Service: after which Commanding Officer inspected the lines.	
	24th		Battalion route march – PROVEN – road E of river HARINGHE – [illegible] at X roads – CROMBEK – cross roads north of LOVIE CHATEAU – PROVEN.	
	25th		Company parades	
	26th		Practice of attack by companies. Alteration in carrying Box respirators.	
	27th		Company training and practice of attack	
	28th		Battalion paraded for special scheme. Baths in the evening. Advance parties went to SOULT FARM to take over accomodation.	
	[illegible]		Inspection at 2.0 pm by G.O.C 4th Div of the Battalion.	

J. P. T. Burchell
2/Lt.

T2134. Wt. W708–776. 500000. 4/15. Sir J. C. & S.

Army Form C. 2118.

Instructions regarding War Diaries and Intelligence Summaries are contained in F. S. Regs., Part II. and the Staff Manual respectively. Title pages will be prepared in manuscript.

WAR DIARY
or
INTELLIGENCE SUMMARY.
(Erase heading not required.)

Place	Date	Hour	Summary of Events and Information	Remarks and references to Appendices
PROVEN	29th		The Battalion proceeded by train at 3 pm for SOULT FARM (B22 b 9.8 1/20000 28 NW) entraining at PROVEN and detraining at ELVERDINGHE.	
SOULT CAMP			Details proceeded by march route to HERZEELE (D10 c 4.8 1/40000 27) A specially detailed party proceeded by march route to DRAGON CAMP (A15 b 2.5 1/20000 28 NW)	
			During night enemy aircraft bombed the area considerably. One casualty occurring at transport	
	30th		Divine service. More raids at night by enemy aircraft. One casualty in our lines	
			J. P. T. Burchell 2/Lt.	

T2134. Wt. W708—776. 500000. 4/15. Sir J. C. & S.

Confidential

10/4

War Diary
— of —
Household Battalion
— from —
1st October 1917
— to —
31st October 1917

Volume 12

[signature]
Major.
for Lieut Colonel
Commanding
Household Battalion

3/11/17

Vol 12

Instructions regarding War Diaries and Intelligence Summaries are contained in F. S. Regs., Part II. and the Staff Manual respectively. Title pages will be prepared in manuscript.

WAR DIARY
or
INTELLIGENCE SUMMARY.
(Erase heading not required.)

Army Form C. 2118.

Place	Date	Hour	Summary of Events and Information	Remarks and references to Appendices
SOULT CAMP Ref Sh 28 N.W. 1/20.000. B23 a 2.3.	1/10/17		2nd Lieuts H G BARKER & A L MARTIN with two platoons sent to 2nd Seaforth Highlrs for ration carrying during forthcoming operations.	
	2/10/17		Working party of 3 officers & 150 O.R under Lieut E S BEECHCROFT carried duckboards under supervision of R.E to the front line.	
	3/10/17		Checking of kit & issue of full battle equipment as laid down in S.S. 135.	
	4/10/17		10th Brigade were left assaulting Brigade of 4th Division. 2nd Seaforth Highlrs assaulting Battn., 3/10th Middlesex in support, 1st R. Warwickshire Regt & Household Battn in Reserve. Zero hour 6 a.m. Attack made by 5th & 2nd Armies.	
IRON CROSS. C 3 a 8.6.			At 7 p.m Battalion moved up to "C" area, H.Q at IRON CROSS C 3 a 8.6. where the Coys dug in for the night. Objectives of 10th Brigade was reported taken. Lt C KENNAWAY & 70 O.R attd to 10th Bde.	
AU BON GITE U29 d 1.9. Ref Sh LANGEMARK 1/10.000.	5th		Battalion (less one company) moved to AU BON GITE at 7.30 P.M. & dug in again. No 1 Coy moved from IRON CROSS at 12 midnight to KANGAROO TRENCH (U24a). There was a light barrage	

T2134. Wt. W708—776. 500000. 4/15. Sir J. C. & S.

Army Form C. 2118.

Instructions regarding War Diaries and Intelligence Summaries are contained in F. S. Regs., Part II. and the Staff Manual respectively. Title pages will be prepared in manuscript.

WAR DIARY
or
INTELLIGENCE SUMMARY.
(Erase heading not required.)

Place	Date	Hour	Summary of Events and Information	Remarks and references to Appendices
			on the line of the STEENBEEK which cost us a few casualties.	
	6th		Intermittent shelling around AU BON GITE.	
LEIPSIG CAMP.	7th		Battalion (less one Coy. in KANGAROO TR.) left AU BON GITE at 12 noon, and returned to LEIPSIG CAMP. Reversion to Winter Time.	
B23a 8.1. Refce. 28 N.W. 1/20000	8th		3 officers + 113 O.R, who have been attached to 9th Field Coy R.E. since the Battalion came into the forward area, rejoined.	
			1 officer + 70 O.R rejoined from 20th D.A.C.	
			1 " + 50 O.R sent to work with 29th D.A.C.	
JOLIE FARM Ref Sh. LANGEMARK 1/10.000 C9a 1.8.			At 6 p.m. Battalion moved to JOLIE FARM (A + B. areas) and dug in. 2/Lts. BARKER + MARTIN + 67 O.R. rejoined.	
	9th		12th Brigade attacked Zero hour 5.20 a.m.	
BIRD HO. U29 b 0.3			At 9 a.m. Battalion moved up in support to the 12th Brigade in the area between BIRD HOUSE (U29 b 0.3 + AU BON GITE) under heavy shell-fire + dug in.	
JOLIE FM.			At 6 p.m. Battalion returned to JOLIE FARM where 1 officer + 50 O.R. lent to 29th D.A.C. rejoined.	
Front line Right Batt. 12th Brigade.	10th		Battalion relieved 2nd ESSEX Regt in the right sub-sector of 12th Brigade front + came under the orders of B.G.C. 12th Bde. We were caught in a heavy barrage on the POELCAPELLE–SCHREIBOOM road on the way up + lost 45 in casualties.	

A7092 Wt. W 5158/M1293 750,000 1/17 D. D. & L. Ltd. Forms/C2118/14.

Instructions regarding War Diaries and Intelligence Summaries are contained in F. S. Regs., Part II. and the Staff Manual respectively. Title pages will be prepared in manuscript.

WAR DIARY
or
INTELLIGENCE SUMMARY.
(Erase heading not required.)

Army Form C. 2118.

Place	Date	Hour	Summary of Events and Information	Remarks and references to Appendices
Front line Right Batt 12th Brigade Ref Sh. BROEMBEEK 1/10.000.	10/10/17.		Relief was complete at 9.30 P.M. It was especially difficult owing to the fact that the line had only been taken up after the attack of the 9th. Batt H.Q at FERDAN HOUSE (U19a 7.5) after relief two front line Coys had to be withdrawn W of POELCAPELLE - LES 5 CHEMINS road owing to heavy artillery shoots.	
	11th		Orders received for the attack to be continued on 12th inst. No movement of troops was possible by day. Coy commanders reconnoitred guiding points for the attack. at 6 p.m. two front line Coys. took up our original front line again 9 P.M. C.O.s conference at Batt H.Q. which all Coy commanders attended.	
	12th		Battalion was in assembly position by 4 a.m 1st R. WARWICKSHIRE Regt on the left 7th R. WEST KENT (18th Div.) on the right. 50 casualties owing to heavy enemy shelling on assembly positions. Zero hour - 5.25 a.m. Battalion attacked on a two Company frontage No. 3 Coy right assaulting Coy No 4 Coy Right Support Coy No. 2 " left " " " 1 " left " "	

A7092. Wt. W5128 g04/1297. 750,000. 1/17. D. D. & L., Ltd. Forms/C2118/14.

Army Form C. 2118.

Instructions regarding War Diaries and Intelligence Summaries are contained in F. S. Regs., Part II. and the Staff Manual respectively. Title pages will be prepared in manuscript.

WAR DIARY
or
INTELLIGENCE SUMMARY.
(Erase heading not required.)

Place	Date	Hour	Summary of Events and Information	Remarks and references to Appendices
	12th		Battalion had two objectives 1st objective. 750 yards to line REQUETE FM. - V14 a 2.8. 2nd " - 1100 " . No's 4 & 1 Coys were to go through No's 3 & 2 after taking the first objective to take the second. Owing to the 18th Division being completely held up in POELCAPELLE we could not go beyond the first objective & a defensive flank towards the village had to be formed. All the officers in No's 2. 3 & 4 Coys became casualties & the line was reorganised as one Coy. by Capt. V.A Cazalet, the only other officer being Lieut L.A Blackburn. The Germans launched a counter-attack on our right flank at 4 P.M. but were easily repulsed. Two platoons of the 1st King's Own reinforced our right flank with one Company of the 1st Rifle Brigade. One Company of 1st Rifle Brigade consolidated a line from LANDING FM. to REQUETE FARM. For full account of operations see APPENDIX "A"	"A"

A7092. Wt. W128 9/M1293 750,000. 1/17. D. D. & L. Ltd. Forms/C2118/14

Army Form C. 2118.

Instructions regarding War Diaries and Intelligence Summaries are contained in F. S. Regs., Part II. and the Staff Manual respectively. Title pages will be prepared in manuscript.

WAR DIARY
or
INTELLIGENCE SUMMARY.
(Erase heading not required.)

Place	Date	Hour	Summary of Events and Information	Remarks and references to Appendices
	12th		25th Northumberland Fusiliers (34th Division) came up to relieve us that night but did not arrive at Battn H.Q. till after midnight & were then very exhausted. It was impossible to complete the relief before daylight, especially as most of our guides had become casualties.	
LEIPSIG CAMP.	13th		Relief was completed at night by 9.15 p.m and Battalion returned to LEIPSIG CAMP. For casualties during the period Oct. 4th - Oct 13th See appendix "B". Total returned from the line 5 officers + 136 O.R.	"B".
PADDOCK WOOD CAMP E4 d & a 9. Ref Sh 27 1/40.000	14th		Battalion entrained at ELVERDINGHE Station at 12 noon + proceeded to PADDOCK WOOD Camp near PROVEN. Reinforcement joined of 7 officers + 241 O.R. from 4th Div. Depot Battn.	
ST JAN TER BIEZEN L2 G1.5	15th		Battalion proceeded by march route to ST JAN TER BIEZEN arriving at 12 noon. Congratulations of Divisional + Army Commanders received on operations of 12th inst.	
	16th		Brigadier General CARTON DE WIART B.G.C. 12th Bde addressed + congratulated the men who have come down from the line. Hon Capt & Quartermaster J.Y. LAUGHTON left the Battalion for duty with the Tank Corps.	

A7092 [illegible]

Army Form C. 2118.

Instructions regarding War Diaries and Intelligence Summaries are contained in F. S. Regs., Part II. and the Staff Manual respectively. Title pages will be prepared in manuscript.

WAR DIARY
or
INTELLIGENCE SUMMARY.
(Erase heading not required.)

Place	Date	Hour	Summary of Events and Information	Remarks and references to Appendices
St JAN TER BIEZEN	17th		Battalion left SCHOOL CAMP at 4 p.m and marched to HOPOUTRE SIDING three miles west of POPERINGHE. Battalion entrained for AUBIGNY at 6 p.m	
DUISANS.	18th		Battalion detrained at AUBIGNY at 5.30 a.m and marched to No 3 UPPER CAMP, DUISANS, arriving there at 8.45 a.m.	
"	19th		Platoon training - specialist classes. Major H.W.S CUNNINGHAME joined the Battalion as 2nd in command.	
"	20th		Platoon football competition.	
"	21st		Memorial service for officers, N.C.O.s & men who fell in action in the recent fighting in FLANDERS. Message of thanks & congratulation received from General GOUGH commanding 5th ARMY for work done whilst serving under his command.	
"	22nd		Platoon training.	
SCHRAMM BARRACKS ARRAS.	23rd		Battalion left No 3 UPPER CAMP, DUISANS at 8.30 a.m and marched to billets in SCHRAMM BARRACKS, ARRAS.	
	24th		Battalion fired musketry course on BUTTE DE TIR range. 10th Brigade took over right sector of 4th Divisional front relieving 37th Brigade - 12th Division, on a one Battalion frontage. 3/10th Middlesex Regt in front, 2nd Seaforth Highlanders in support, 1st R. Warwickshire Regt & Household Battn in Reserve.	

R. [illegible] Dill
Captain & Adjutant

A5834 Wt. W4973/M687 750,000 8/16 D. D. & L. Ltd. Forms/C.2118/13.

Instructions regarding War Diaries and Intelligence Summaries are contained in F. S. Regs., Part II. and the Staff Manual respectively. Title pages will be prepared in manuscript.

WAR DIARY
or
INTELLIGENCE SUMMARY.
(Erase heading not required.)

Army Form C. 2118.

Place	Date	Hour	Summary of Events and Information	Remarks and references to Appendices
COLLEGE COMMUNALE ARRAS	25th		Platoon training.	
			Battalion moved from SCHRAMM BARRACKS to COLLEGE COMMUNALE RUE D'ARSENAL at 2 P.M.	
	26th		Platoon training.	
	27th		His Eminence Cardinal Bourne addressed all Roman Catholics at 4P.M.	
	28th		Divine Service.	
			Lewis Gunners fired a course on the MOAT RANGE, ARRAS	
			Reinforcement of 216 O.R. arrived at 4th Div. Depot Battn. SAVY.	
	29th		Platoon training.	
			Draft inspected by C.O. at SAVY.	
	30th		Platoon Training.	
			The Company Commanders reconnoitred our sector of the line.	
	31st		The Battalion had the use of the baths in SCHRAMM BARRACKS.	
			Reinforcement of 216 joined the Battalion from the 4th Div Depot.	
			H. J. Thomas. 2nd Lieut. & Asst Adjt. Household Battalion	

A5834 Wt. W4973 M687 750,000 8/16 D. D. & L. Ltd. Forms/C.2118/13.

Summary of the Household Battalion from Oct 4 - Oct 14

Oct 4. The Battalion (minus 3 platoons) was in Reserve at South Camp, 3 platoons being attached to the 9th Field Co until Oct. 10th. During this time they made thirty two journeys from the Canal to EAGLE TRENCH.
While the other two platoons carried the whole of the rations & ammunition up to the Seaforths in the front line.
At 6 pm Oct. 5th the Batt. was ordered to move to IRON CROSS AREA and arrived there in support at 11 pm, the men being in shell holes and digging themselves in.

Oct 6. At 6 pm we received orders to go up in close support to AU BON GITE and one COMPANY to be lent to the ROYAL WARWICKSHIRE REGT. as support Co in KANGAROO TRENCH. The Battn arrived at AU BON GITE at 10 pm and dug themselves in.

Oct 6 Battalion remained at AU BON GITE, one Coy. still being in KANGAROO TRENCH.

Oct 7 Battalion left AU BON GITE at 12 noon and returned to LEIPZIG CAMP. The Coy from KANGAROO TRENCH returned at 4.30 am on the morning of Oct. 8th.

Oct 8 At 6 pm. Battalion proceeded to STRAY FARM AREA men digging themselves in.

Oct 9 At 10 am Battalion ordered up to AU BON GITE in support to the 12th Brigade, arrived there 12 noon under heavy shell fire, men dug in there. At 6 pm we received orders to return to STRAY FARM AREA arrived there at 10 pm.

Oct 10. Received orders to go up the same evening to take over from 2nd ESSEX Regt. as right Battn of the 12th Brigade to take part in the attack which was to be continued on the 9th. Commanding Officer & Company Commanders went forward to make arrangements for relief.
Up to this date our casualties had been 43 O.R.
At 4 30 pm the first Company left STRAY FARM AREA, arriving at the ESSEX Hqrs. at FERDAN HOUSE at 7 pm, on the way up the Battn. had to pass through a heavy barrage on POELCAPELLE – SCHREIBOOM ROAD and had 45 casualties. Relief was complete by 9.30 pm, this relief was a very difficult one as the line had only been taken up on the 9th. To make things harder we had to withdraw our two front Coys. at 4 am. to

the shell hole W of POELCAPELLE – LES CINQ-CHEMINS ROAD to enable the heavy artillery to have a destructive shoot, at the same time marking their former positions so that they could take them up again the following evening.

Oct 11. Operation Orders received for the attack 12 noon, as men had to keep perfectly still by daytime, Company Commanders + Hqrs. spent their time in making out landmarks for the attack + trying to see the ground. At 5pm orders received cancelling the KING'S OWN taking the second objective + leaving the whole of the right flank two objectives to the Household Bn. I pointed out that with the men tired this might be difficult but there were no other troops available.
At 6pm Companies took up their former positions again in the front shell hole system. At 7pm Companies with Company Commanders went through operat orders very carefully, laying stress on the following points

(1) I felt certain that POELCAPELLE would be very dangerous and that my right Companies if necessary were to start forming a defensive flank at once.

(2) If POELCAPELLE did not fall REQUETTE FARM would be as far as our right flank could go, and we would pivot on that.

(3) The two machine guns attached to us would go with the right assaulting Coy. + right support Co and would eventually make a strong point at REQUETTE FARM facing S.E. + S.W.

(4) Information was to be sent at 4 different stages of the attack.

Our Assembly position was 150 yds E of POELCAPELLE CINQ CHEMINS ROAD.

500 yds frontage
1st objective 750 yds
2nd " 1100 "

1st King's Own (2 Coys. in Support)
1st Rifle Brigade (2 " " Reserve)

1st. ROYAL WARWICKSHIRE on our left ROYAL WEST KENT'S (18th Division) on our right.
We lined up with our right on a flag marked out by the 18th Div. at 4 am.
In the meantime owing to heavy shelling we had had 50 more casualties.

Oct. 12 The Battn in assembly position at 4am where an extra ration of rum was issued. the West Kents had not finished lining up till 5.15 am.

ZERO HOUR 5·25 am Hqrs. R.W.K. moved to FERDAN HOUSE with me while I was also in telephone communication with Hqrs. Kings Own Regt.

First Message received from left support Coy at 6.10 am to say left Coy on first objective and in [illegible] on the left.

Second Message 6.40 am right Company Commander returned wounded reported right Coy. within 50 yds of REQUETTE FARM but not in touch on right so defensive flank was being formed. All the casualties occurred on right from heavy machine gun fire from POELCAPELLE.

Third Message 6.50 am Report from my forward observing Officer at STRING HOUSES to say that the whole of our first objective had been taken including REQUETTE FARM.

Fourth Message. 7.20 am. LEFT Support Coy 300 yds E. of LANDING FARM, 4 Machine guns + 26 prisoners captured in REQUETTE FARM (these guns were 30 yds W. of the FARM and were destroyed by Capt Cazalet)

* REQUETTE FARM consisted of a small broken down Pill BOX used by the Germans as a dressing station and surrounded of the W by a marsh and S.E under hostile fire from some trees with a small dip or trench this side of them which made it difficult to hold.

Fifth Message. 9.30 am received from left Support Company Commander, he was in touch with my right support Company Commander (All the Officers in my two Companies having become casualties) No touch could be got with WEST KENTS. two platoons already detailed and forming a defensive flank.

Another Strong Point E of LANDING FARM had yielded 23 more prisoners: over 100 prisoners had already been taken by the Battalion. More S.A.A. required (owing to heavy casualties companies had been ~~formed~~ formed into 2. My right being under Lieut Davies, Lieut Marten in the centre, Capt Cazalet on my left) Not having sufficient men have put 40 men between WARWICKS and ourselves.

At 7.50 am I had asked O.C. Kings Own to detach two platoons to prolong my defensive flank and repeated this to Capt Cazalet to make full use of them when reorganizing.

Sixth Message. 9.55 am received No. 4 Coy consolidating on the REQUETTE FARM objective two platoons forming a defensive flank

Signed Lieut Davies

Seventh Message 9.55 am received. Remains of No 3 Coy consolidating to the left of Lieut. Davies and right of Capt Cazalet on the first objective. Signed Lieut Martin

10.50 am. Following message sent to Lieut. Davies

"REQUETTE FARM to be held at all costs."

(Both my Vickers Guns having been destroyed)

I hope to be able to send you up two more machine guns

11 am S.A.A. to be collected from casualties. REQUETTE FARM to be held.

In the meantime the intelligence Officer had been up to the line, and reported REQUETTE FARM not to be held, our men being 50 yds W.

11.20 am received orders from 12th Brigade to say we were to be relieved that night

Divisional Machine Gun Officer also arrived. Sent him to try and find position for his guns near REQUETTE FARM.

3.40 pm Message received from Capt Cazalet. REQUETTE FARM. GERMANS surround it on all sides except N.W. it would be useless to advance we had to retire from it to hill just below and prolong our defensive flank.

3.30 pm 5 Hqt. Runners sent up as guides to learn the way for relief, all became casualties, being sniped from POELCAPELLE.

3 pm Intense shelling in FERDAN HOUSE AREA lasting 3 hours.

4 pm 7 guides sent to Brigade Hqts. to act as guides to incoming Battn. 2 became casualties

4.15 pm Message received.

"REQUETTE FARM must be captured by this evening, you will arrange with Rifle Brigade to support you."

O.C. Rifle Brigade sent his Adjutant over to arrange for 2 platoons from his right Co. to support, but found it too weak owing to casualties to assist.

Sent message to Capt Cazalet to take REQUETTE FARM but he had so few men left, and only one Officer who was suffering from exposure that he was unable to carry this out.

3 pm A counter attack on our left front and the Warwick right was repulsed

Household Battalion Operation Orders No 31.
[illegible] 11th 1917

APPENDIX 'A'

1. The attack will be continued on Z day.

2. (a) The 12th INF. BDE. is carrying out the attack on the 4th Divisional front.

(b) The 18th Div is attacking on the right
17th " " " left.

3. The Brigade will attack on a two Battalion frontage
Dispositions as follows —

Right Assaulting Batt.	Household Bn.
Left " "	2nd R. WARWICKSHIRE REGT.
Brigade support	2nd Duke of Wellington's Regt. [illegible]
" reserve	1st Rifle Bde

4. 1 Section (2 guns) of 10th M.G. Coy will be at the disposal of O.C. Household Battn. These will be allotted to Nos. 3 & 4 Coys. (right assaulting Coys).

5. Household Battn. will be right assaulting Batt. of 12th Brigade
Dispositions as follows —

Right Assaulting Coy	No 3 Coy
Left "	No 2 "
Right Support	" 4 "
Left "	" 1 "

6. Boundaries between Coys & Battns. as shown on Maps already issued

7 Coys will attack on two platoon frontage according to formation A

8 Objectives

There will be two objectives

GREEN LINE } as shown
RED " } on map

9 GUIDING POINTS must be found and pointed out to all subordinate Commanders

i.e. Right Coys. – REQUETTE FARM
Left " – LANDING FARM

10 Assembly positions

(a) Nos 3 & 2 Coys will form up 130 yds N.E. of POELCAPELLE – LES 5 CHEMINS road

(b) Nos. 4 & 1 Coys will form 50 yds N.E. of road mentioned in (a)

All Coys will be in position by Zero minus two hours

(c) Two Coys of the KING'S OWN will form up in Support S.W. of road

11 Barrage

[illegible] barrage is shown in blue on the map.

Barrage will commence to creep at Zero + 8 minutes and will move forward at the rate of 100 yds in 5 minutes to the GREEN line when it will halt till Zero + [illegible] minutes when it will move forward again at the same rate.

A few smoke shells will be fired

when it commences to advance from the Green line. On reaching the RED LINE it will form a protective barrage.

12 (a) At Zero hour HOUSEHOLD BN. will advance. Nos 3 & 2 Coys. will capture the GREEN LINE and consolidate it.

(b) At Zero + [illegible] when the Barrage commences to advance Nos 1 & 4 Coys. will go through No 2 & 3 & will capture the RED LINE. Nos 2 & 3 Coys. following [illegible] Coys.

(c) Consolidation will be carried out immediately RED LINE is captured. Posts of Lewis Guns & riflemen will be pushed out not more than 100 yds to the front to cover consolidation which will be carried out in depth.

13. Counter-attack Coys.

Nos. 1 & 4 Coys will be counter attack Coys till the GREEN line is reached. Nos 2 & 3 Coys. will be counter attack Coys. from the Green line to the Red line.

14. Liaison

(a) 1 NCO & 3 men will be told off from Nos 3 & 2 Coys. to keep touch with Battns on right & left respectively. These parties will continue liaison duties as far as the RED LINE

(b) In the event of either flank being held up, the support platoon on the outer flank of Nos 2 & 3 Coy must be detailed to be in readiness to form a defensive flank.

(c) Touch must be maintained with the flanks of all costs.

(d) O.C. No 3 Coy will get into touch with 18th Division at REGUETTE FARM. Runners for this post must be detailed beforehand.

15. Mopping up parties will be told off beforehand as follows:—

No 3 Coy.	STRING HOUSES
	REGUETTE FARM
No 2 Coy	LANDING FARM
	HUTS V.14 a 5.3.

16. Aeroplanes.

(a) Contact aeroplanes will fly over at
Zero + 1 hr 15 mins
" + 3 hrs 30 mins
12 noon.

Red flares will be lit by leading troops on being called for by KLAXON horn or white lights.

(b) Counter-attack aeroplane will be in the air continuously during daylight to detect the approach of enemy counter attacks.

17. Battn. HQ will remain at Ferdan House until Green Line is captured when they will move to STRING HOUSES - then to LANDING FARM or [illegible] FARM.

18. Report to be sent to Battn. HQ as soon as possible.
A representative will be left at FERDAN HOUSE to forward reports in event of Battn HQ having moved.
In every case reports must include statement as to whether touch has been kept on right & left.

19. Substitutes for Company, platoon and section commanders must be thoroughly acquainted with the plan of attack.

20. All ranks must remember that in this form of warfare the most effective form of support is in most cases given by outflanking the enemy rather than by giving more weight to the attack as one does in trench warfare.

21. TIME Representatives from each Coy will be sent to Battn HQ at 9 pm to synchronise watches.

22. AID POST will remain at FERDAN HOUSE

23. PRISONERS will be sent to Battn HQ

24. Z day will be October 12th.

25. Zero hour to be notified later.

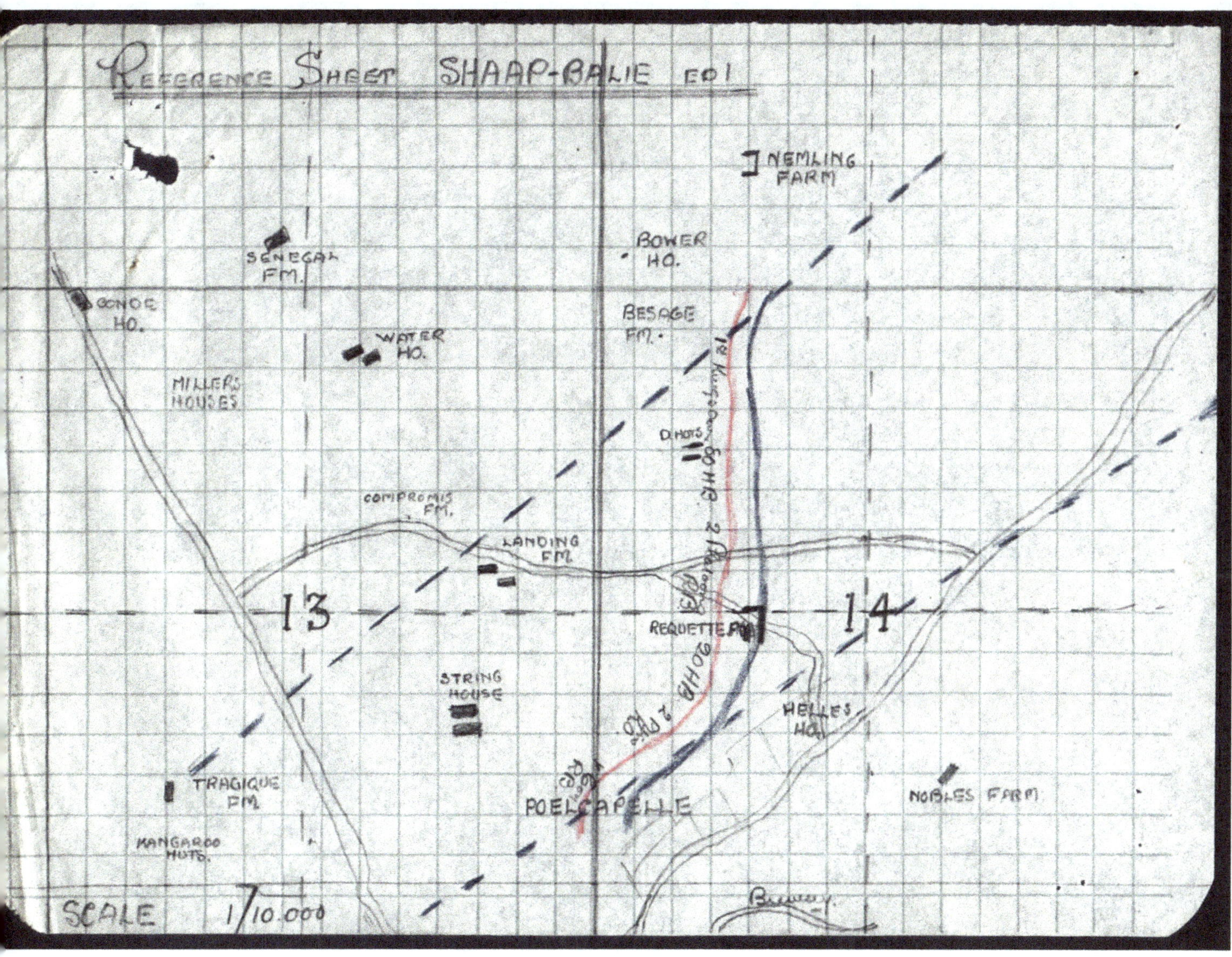
REFERENCE SHEET SHAAP-BALIE EO1
NEMLING FARM
BOWER HO.
SENEGAL FM.
GONOE HO.
BESAGE FM.
WATER HO.
MILLERS HOUSES
D. HOTS
COMPROMIS FM.
LANDING FM.
13
14
REQUETTE FM
STRING HOUSE
HELLES HO.
TRAGIQUE FM
POELCAPELLE
NOBLES FARM
KANGAROO HUTS
SCALE 1/10.000

SKETCH MAP

Shewing Positions

Captured and held by

HOUSEHOLD BATTN.
on October 12th 1917.

Blue line shows position at 9 am.

Red line shows position finally consolidated and handed over.

Blue dotted line shows Battn. Boundaries.

5 pm A counter attack from REQUETTE FARM was launched, 2 platoons Rifle Brigade came up and drove them back.

At 6 pm. the situation was as follows (map attached) Royal Warwickshire holding the left, 40 men Kings Own on their right, about 100 men of the H.B. holding the front to a point W. of REQUETTE FARM, 2 platoons of R.B. holding the portion of flank now facing REQUETTE FARM, then 20 or 30 men H.B. all that remained of No 4 Coy facing S. towards POELCAPELLE 2 platoons Kings Own on their right, 1 Coy Rifle Brigade on the extreme right joining up with the Suffolks who had relieved the WEST KENTS.

The O.C. Kings Own & Rifle Brigade were in touch with me the whole time.

The relieving unit 25 N.F. did not arrive till 2.30 am their men being in great coats and very tired. I saw that it would be impossible to carry out the relief as a whole that night.

I sent one Co. with my Adjutant and a guide from the R.B. to relieve 1 Co. R.B. on my extreme right flank, another Co. to relieve 2 platoons Kings Own & my own 20 men on the East of them all on the defensive flank, this Co. was conducted by my Regimental Sergeant Major who worked on a compass bearing & striking a point 50 yds W. of REQUETTE FARM: the Kings Own were not relieved as 2 platoons of the relieving Co went wrong, the other Co. I sent to act as support to Capt Cazalet their left being on LANDING FARM and stretching in S.E. direction. I took out the other Coy myself and placed them 250 yds E of POELCAPELLE - CINQ CHEMINS ROADS to avoid the Barrage lines.

My men were without rations or water as we had hoped to have relieved them.

All our runners except 2 had become casualties.

Oct 13th. At 6 am. I went up to the left of our line and saw Capt Cazalet and found that the 2 platoons of R.B. were in touch on the right with the N.F. just in front of REQUETTE FARM, as I was not quite certain of the situation there, I also arranged with him that the Coy of N.F in support at LANDING FARM should relieve him & the 2 platoons of the Rifle Brigade on his right.

I also arranged with O.C. N.F. to relieve Kings Own who were between his two Companies on the defensive flank

On 12th I sent up my intelligence and signalling Officer to help Capt. Cazalet as he had no Officer left no Corporal Major & only 2 Corporals of Horse. My intelligence officer was also wounded.
Relief was complete by 9.15 pm
We returned to LIEPZIG CAMP
On Oct 10th we went up 498 O.R.
" " with at present we only have 150 O.R.

348 Casualties
43
391 Casualties since Oct 4.

Officers 4 Killed
9 Wounded
13

Only Capt. Cazalet & Lieut. Blackburn left & Officers on Battn. Hqrs.

The casualties occurred through taking an objective of 600 yds. and forming a defensive flank from the actual start.
I cannot speak too highly of the conduct of the Officers & men as they were tired when they went in and were wet through and subject to heavy shelling for 24 hours before the start.
Capt. Cazalet's work is deserving of the highest praise he led the attack with great gallantry & reorganized the whole of the line himself quite alone. I should not think a finer bit of work has been done by anyone during this war.
Capt Sloan M.C. our doctor dressed 150 cases under very heavy shell fire.
While I should like to mention the work done by my Adjutant & RSM in helping with a very difficult relief. Our officers & NCO casualties speak for themselves and shew with what great gallantry they all helped to gain a very difficult objective. The Battalion took at least 100 prisoners and 4 machine guns.
The information sent back during these operations was especially good.
The direction kept in the attack was also good.
The pause of 45 minutes on the Green line was too long.
The forming of the defensive flank was

carried out by the two right support companies. As usual the difficulty arose when all the Officers except one became casualties. I should like always to have Officers to send up at the end of an attack as that is the time extra energy and organization is required.

APPENDIX "B"

Casualties from 4th to 13th October 1917.

Officers

Lieut C. G. Kennaway Wounded 10-10-17
2/Lieut H. J. Kennaway " 11-10-17.
Lieut L. Scott. Killed 12-10-17
2/Lt O. Wakefield " "
Lieut C. S. Beachcroft " "
2/Lt L. J. Stockwood D of W "
Capt J. Moffat Wounded "
2/Lt H. S. Blackburn " "
" H. J. Barker M.C " "
" C. H. Davies " "
Lieut P. C. Trotter " "
2/Lieut A. G. Barnard " "
" G. L. Whitelaw " "

Other Ranks

Killed	54
D of Wds	11
Wounded	278
missing	40
" believed Killed	7
Wounded & missing	4
Total Casualties	394

APPENDIX "A"

List of Honours & Awards
between 4th and 14th October 1917

				Awarded
6711	C of M	PAYNE. A.W.	Military Medal	25. 10. 17
1643	"	HARRINGTON. H.J.	" "	25. 10. 17
15	"	READ. V. H.	" "	25. 10. 17
2294	a/Cpl	MATTHEWS. E.C.	" "	25. 10. 17
457	2/Pte	SPALDING A.H.	" "	25. 10. 17
267	"	PORTER. H	" "	25. 10. 17
538	"	WARNER.	" "	25. 10. 17
1455	"	A.W. GLASS	" "	25. 10. 17
1735	"	E.W. PEACH. (att 10th T.M.B)	" "	25. 10. 17

T/2/Lieut	MARTIN. A.L.	MILITARY CROSS.	17. 10. 17.
Lt.-Col.	W.R. PORTAL.	D.S.O.	1 - 11 - 17
Capt	J.F.M. Sloan M.C. RAMC	Bar to M.C.	1. 11. 17
Capt	V.A. CAZALET	MILITARY CROSS.	1. 11. 17
2/Lieut	C.H. DAVIES	" "	1. 11. 17
2575 R.C.M.	WRIGHT. C	D.C.M.	1. 11. 17
717. C of H	BISHOP. H.T.	"	1. 11. 17
2808 Tpr	LANGLEY. C.F	"	1. 11. 17

Confidential

War Diary
of
Household Battalion
from
1st November 1917
to
30th November 1917

Volume 13.

3/12/17.

R. J. Sith
Captain & Adjt.
for Lieut. Colonel

Vol 13

Instructions regarding War Diaries and Intelligence Summaries are contained in F. S. Regs., Part II. and the Staff Manual respectively. Title pages will be prepared in manuscript.

WAR DIARY
or
INTELLIGENCE SUMMARY.
(Erase heading not required.)

Army Form C. 2118.

Place	Date	Hour	Summary of Events and Information	Remarks and references to Appendices
COLLEGE COMMUNALE ARRAS.	1st NOV.		Battalion left COLLEGE COMMUNALE, ARRAS at 2.30 P.M and marched to the front line taking over 10th Brigade Sector from 2nd SEAFORTH HIGHLRS. Relief complete without casualty at 9.15 P.M.	
Front line CAMBRAI ROAD Sector			Dispositions. No's 2 & 1 Coys in the line No's 3 & 4 " " Support.	
014a 6.7 – 086 2.1 (Ref Sh. 51b S.W. 1/20.000)			Battalion H Q at CRATER SUBWAY in GORDON AVENUE.	
	2nd		Organised trench mortar shoot on German trenches.	
	3rd		Quiet day. Patrol under Lieut. ROBERTS located German machine gun emplacement – was out reconnoitring enemy wire from 6.0 p.m – 7.33 p.m. Inter Company relief carried out No. 4 Coy relieved No. 1 Coy in right sub-sector " 3 " " " 2 " left " "	
	4th		Quiet day.	
	5th		Battalion relieved by 1st R. WARWICKSHIRE Regt. Relief complete without casualty at 4.45 P.M. The whole relief was completed by daylight. During this tour in the line, working parties of 60 O.R. have been found daily on revetting & duckboarding the front line. 90 yards of this were completed in four days and in addition the whole of Saps 2 & 3. Parties for carrying material were found nightly. The work was conducted under the supervision ~~of the~~ O.C. 9th Field Coy R.E who sent in a report to Brigade H.Q that the work	

Instructions regarding War Diaries and Intelligence Summaries are contained in F. S. Regs., Part II. and the Staff Manual respectively. Title pages will be prepared in manuscript.

WAR DIARY
or
INTELLIGENCE SUMMARY.
(Erase heading not required.)

Army Form C. 2118.

Place	Date	Hour	Summary of Events and Information	Remarks and references to Appendices
			done had been worthy of the highest praise & had exceeded all expectation.	
			On relief the Battalion moved into Brigade Support with two Companies (No's 3 & 4) in SPADE RESERVE & two Companies (No's 1 & 2) & Battn HQ at LES FOSSES FARM, where the accomodation is in large excavated caverns 40 feet under the ground.	
LES FOSSES FARM N11 G 9.4 (Ref Sh 51 b S.W. 1/20.000)	6th		Further list of awards received including Lieut. Col W. R. PORTAL awarded D.S.O. Capt. V. A. CAZALET " M.C 2nd Lieut. C. H. DAVIES " M.C. Capt. J. F. M. SLOAN M.C R.A.M.C " Bar to M.C.	
			For full list of awards for period Oct. 4th - 14th see appendix "A"	"A".
			Two American officers attached for instruction.	
			Working parties - By day ... 32 O.R. By night .. 6 officers + 258 O.R.	
	7th		Working parties as on 6th	
	8th		" " " " "	
	9th		Working party of 30 found in the morning.	
			Battalion was relieved by 2nd SEAFORTH HIGHLRS. Relief complete at 9.30 P.M	
			On relief Battalion moved to Brigade Reserve in the BROWN LINE	
			Casualties during tour in the line - 4 O.R. wounded.	R. W. Dill Capt + adjt.

(A7092). Wt. W12839/M1293. 750,000. 1/17. D. D. & L., Ltd. Forms/C.2118/14.

Army Form C. 2118.

Instructions regarding War Diaries and Intelligence Summaries are contained in F. S. Regs., Part II. and the Staff Manual respectively. Title pages will be prepared in manuscript.

WAR DIARY
or
INTELLIGENCE SUMMARY.
(Erase heading not required.)

Place	Date	Hour	Summary of Events and Information	Remarks and references to Appendices
BROWN LINE N.10 a.	10th		Owing to rain in the night many of the shelters in the trenches fell in, & owing to the mud conditions became bad. It is not possible to do much concerted training owing to the high level of the ground rendering observation of troops easy to the enemy, & to number of men required for working parties. Company strengths were therefore reduced to 60, the surplus were sent to details at SCHRAMM BARRACKS.	
	11th		All men employed on working parties in the front & support lines by night.	
	12th		Working parties found as on 11th.	

[illegible signature]

(A7092). Wt. W12839/M1293. 750,000. 1/17. D. D. & L., Ltd. Forms/C.2118/14.

Instructions regarding War Diaries and Intelligence Summaries are contained in F. S. Regs., Part II. and the Staff Manual respectively. Title pages will be prepared in manuscript.

WAR DIARY
or
INTELLIGENCE SUMMARY.
(Erase heading not required.)

Army Form C. 2118.

Place	Date	Hour	Summary of Events and Information	Remarks and references to Appendices
BROWN LINE.	Nov 13th		Major W. W. SMITH CUNINGHAME 2nd in Command of the Battalion and 2nd Lieut H. J. THOMAS assistant adjutant changed places with Lieut. Col. W. S. PORTAL DSO and Capt. R. W. DILL who went back to the Details in ARRAS. Working and Carrying parties of 2 officers and 118 O.R. were furnished for work on the front line & carrying up R.E. material and T.M. bombs.	
	14th		The same working parties were supplied as on the previous day and in addition a further party of 48 men were furnished for carrying up T.M. bombs.	
	15th		Working parties as on the 13th and a further party of 48 to carry T.M. bombs.	
	16th	10am	Lieut. SANDFORD and 2nd Lieut E. N. de GEIJER and 40 men from Details met the Div. Gas Officer at ESTAMINET CORNER (H.31.b.25.00.) and were taught to throw smoke bombs. The same working parties as before were supplied. Capt HALL R.A.M.C. was attached to us temporarily as M.O. The strength of the Coys was made up to 95 O.R. each from Details.	
Front line CAMBRAI ROAD Sector O.14.a.6.7.–O.8.b.2.1 Ref Sheet 51b S.W 1/20,000	17th		Battalion left the BROWN LINE and marched to the front line taking over the 10th Brigade Sector from the 2nd Seaforth Highlanders. Relief complete at 8.15 pm. Dispositions No 3 & 4 Coys in the line No 1 & 2 —— support. Batt. H.Q at CRATER SUBWAY in GORDON AVENUE. 2nd Lieut E.N. de GEIJER received a scalp wound during the bombardment following a raid by the Division on our left but remained at duty. A Lewis Gun post was blown up by a trench mortar and 1 Cpl was killed, two men wounded.	[illegible signature]

(A7092). Wt. W12839/M1293. 75,000. 1/17. D. D. & L., Ltd. Forms/C.2118/14.

Instructions regarding War Diaries and Intelligence Summaries are contained in F. S. Regs., Part II. and the Staff Manual respectively. Title pages will be prepared in manuscript.

WAR DIARY
or
INTELLIGENCE SUMMARY.
(Erase heading not required.)

Army Form C. 2118.

Place	Date	Hour	Summary of Events and Information	Remarks and references to Appendices
Front LINE.	18	3 pm	A bombardment of the enemy's line in the MONCHY sector took place, in conjunction with which 30 men of the Battalion under Lieut V. H. SANDFORD and 2nd Lieut. E.N. de GEIJER threw out smoke bombs from the right half of our front line. The whole of the front line was cleared during the bombardment except for 8 Lewis Gun post, the garrison being kept in the dugouts in the support line. The enemy retaliated with a considerable barrage both of light artillery and trench mortars but no casualties were caused.	
	19th		Inter Coy relief carried out No 1 Coy relieved No 3 2 ——— 4.	
			At 7. pm. Lieut J. P. NIVEN with a party from No 1 Coy began to cut five gaps in our own wire between 0.8.b.2.1 and 0.8.d.0.7 in preparation for the raid by the 1st R Warwickshire Regt. This task took about 4 hours. During this night 45 dummy figures were carried up GORDON AVENUE and put out under Lieut BLACKBURN in front of our front line from the CAMBRAI Road to about 0.14.b.1.9. 1000 smoke candles & 500 P. bombs were carried up GORDON AVENUE & distributed along the front line trench.	
	20th		At 6.20 am the 1st R. Warwickshire Regt made a very successful raid, starting	[illegible signature]

(A7092). Wt. W12839/M1293. 75,000. 1/17. D. D. & L., Ltd. Forms/C.2118/14.

Instructions regarding War Diaries and Intelligence Summaries are contained in F. S. Regs., Part II. and the Staff Manual respectively. Title pages will be prepared in manuscript.

WAR DIARY
or
INTELLIGENCE SUMMARY.
(Erase heading not required.)

Army Form C. 2118.

Place	Date	Hour	Summary of Events and Information	Remarks and references to Appendices
FRONT LINE	20th contd		through the gaps cut in our wire. In conjunction with this raid Lieut BLACKBURN and 20 men from No 2 Coy raised the dummy figures at 6.20 am. These drew heavy fire from the enemy and achieved their object. Lieut. V. H. SANDFORD and 20 men were prepared to throw out the smoke candles and P bombs, but as the wind was unfavourable this was abandoned. At 7. am, after the raiding party had returned, Lieut J. P. NIVEN with a party from No 1 Coy successfully filled the gaps cut in our own wire, during which operation he & 1 O.R. were wounded.	
			The Brigadier General commanding the 10th Infantry Brigade congratulated the Battalion upon the highly successful way in which the dummies had been manipulated & the smoke discharged, contributing to the success of the raid.	
			As it was thought possible that owing to operations elsewhere the enemy might fall back from his present position, a patrol under Corpl H. Newman was sent out at 6. pm to find out if his trenches were still occupied. A second patrol under 2nd Lieut WHITEHOUSE went out at 2 am the next morning with the same object. Both patrols reported that the enemy were present & observed signs of work going on.	[illegible]

(A7092). Wt. W12839/M1293. 750,000. 1/17. D. D. & L., Ltd. Forms/C.2118/14.

Instructions regarding War Diaries and Intelligence Summaries are contained in F. S. Regs., Part II. and the Staff Manual respectively. Title pages will be prepared in manuscript.

WAR DIARY
or
INTELLIGENCE SUMMARY.
(Erase heading not required.)

Army Form C. 2118.

Place	Date	Hour	Summary of Events and Information	Remarks and references to Appendices
FRONT LINE.	21.		During the night of the 20th/21st the dummies were brought in & they & the smoke bombs carried out of the trenches.	
			The Battalion was relieved by the 1st R. Warwickshire Regt. Relief was complete by 4. pm. The work in the line was interrupted by the Smoke discharge & the Raid. but every day parties worked under the R. E. revetting the front line.	
			On relief the Battalion moved into Brigade Support with two companies No 1 & 2 in SPADE RESERVE & two Coys No 3 & 4 & Batt. H.Q at	
LES FOSSES FARM.	22.		LES FOSSES FARM. Working parties. Morning. 84. O.R. Evening 1 Off & 110. O.R.	
	23		Working parties as on 22nd.	
	24.		ditto	
	25.		Working party of 84 in the morning. Battalion was relieved by 2/10 Middlesex Regt. Relief complete by 7.15. pm. On relief Battalion marched to ECOLE COMMUNAL in ARRAS in Brigade Reserve.	

A7092. Wt. W128 9/M1293 750,000. 1/17. D. D & L., Ltd. Forms C2118/14.

Instructions regarding War Diaries and Intelligence Summaries are contained in F. S. Regs., Part II. and the Staff Manual respectively. Title pages will be prepared in manuscript.

WAR DIARY
or
INTELLIGENCE SUMMARY.

(Erase heading not required.)

Army Form C. 2118.

Place	Date	Hour	Summary of Events and Information	Remarks and references to Appendices
COLLEGE COMMUNALE	26th	inst	Platoon Training and Checking Equipment.	
ARRAS	27th		Company Training according to Training Scheme.	
COLLEGE COMMUNALE and BOIS DES BOEUFS. N.2.a.	28th		Owing to the 61st Division being moved to another part of the front, further south, the Household Battalion was suddenly called upon to go into Reserve at BOIS DES BOEUFS, while the 10th Brigade put 2 Battalions into the front line instead of the usual 1. Details, including Lewis Gun Classes, were left at the SCHRAMM Barracks, ARRAS, under the 2nd in Command Major Smith Cunninghame.	
	29th		Two Companies carried out training on the BEAURAINS ROAD. Two Companies supplied large working parties preparing for a Trench	

A7092. Wt. W1125 9/M1293. 750,000. 1/17. D. D & L., Ltd. Forms/C. 2118/14.

Instructions regarding War Diaries and Intelligence Summaries are contained in F. S. Regs., Part II. and the Staff Manual respectively. Title pages will be prepared in manuscript.

WAR DIARY
or
INTELLIGENCE SUMMARY.
(Erase heading not required.)

Army Form C. 2118.

Place	Date	Hour	Summary of Events and Information	Remarks and references to Appendices
	29th cont.		Mortar Shoot due to come off shortly. 1 Platoon made 60 coils of concertina wire and delivered it at the R.E. Dump near LES FOSSES FARM.	
	30th inst.		Training was again carried out by 2 companies while the other 2 Companies supplied working and carrying parties. 60 coils of concertina wire were again made and delivered. St Andrews day was celebrated by a Scottish Concert in the Church Army Hut in the Camp.	

A7092 Wt. W128 9/M1293 750,000. 1/17. D. D & L., Ltd. Forms/C2118/14.

Army Form C. 2118.

Instructions regarding War Diaries and Intelligence Summaries are contained in F. S. Regs., Part II. and the Staff Manual respectively. Title pages will be prepared in manuscript.

WAR DIARY
or
INTELLIGENCE SUMMARY.

(Erase heading not required.)

Place	Date	Hour	Summary of Events and Information	Remarks and references to Appendices
BOIS DES BOEUFS CAMP	30th		Working party of 225 found for carrying up T M ammunition. Party complimented on its work by G O C 4th Division. 60 coils of concertina wire made & sent up daily to front line	

R. J. Dill
Capt & Adjt

A7092 Wt. W125 9/M1293 750,000 6/17 D. D & L. Ltd. Forms C. 2118/14.

Confidential

War Diary
of
Household Battalion
— from —
1st December 1917,
— to —
31st December 1917

Volume. 14

W.M. Portal
Lieut Colonel
Commanding
Household Battn

3-1-18

14

Instructions regarding War Diaries and Intelligence Summaries are contained in F. S. Regs., Part II. and the Staff Manual respectively. Title pages will be prepared in manuscript.

WAR DIARY
or
INTELLIGENCE SUMMARY.
(Erase heading not required.)

Army Form C. 2118.

Place	Date	Hour	Summary of Events and Information	Remarks and references to Appendices
BOIS DES BOEUFS.	1st DECEMBER		Working and Carrying Parties as on the previous nights 60 coils of concertina wire were again made and delivered	
BOIS DES BOEUFS and COLLEGE COMMUNAL ARRAS.	2nd		The Battalion was relieved in the afternoon by the 2nd Battn of the Duke of Wellington's WEST RIDING Regiment, and marched by Companies to the COLLEGE COMMUNAL in ARRAS	
	3rd		In accordance with Battalion Scheme of Training, training was carried out near the BUTTE DE TIR and the Coys fired on the Range Arr. In the afternoon Coy Commanders took their N.C.O.s out along the ACHICOURT Road and went over with them the ground on which a Field Firing Practise was to be carried out on the morrow	
	4th		The Battalion carried out a Field Firing Practise by half-Battalions on an area south of ACHICOURT at 51 b S.W. M.2. Lewis Gunners and Rifle	

A7092 Wt. [illegible] 750000 1/17 D. D. & L. Ltd. Forms C2118/14

Instructions regarding War Diaries and Intelligence Summaries are contained in F. S. Regs., Part II. and the Staff Manual respectively. Title pages will be prepared in manuscript.

WAR DIARY
or
INTELLIGENCE SUMMARY.
(Erase heading not required.)

Army Form C. 2118.

Place	Date	Hour	Summary of Events and Information	Remarks and references to Appendices
COLLEGE COMMUNALE ARRAS	4th DEC cont		Bombers cooperated with ~~the~~ Riflemen. The practise was carried out under the inspection of the Divisional G.S.O 1	
	5th		Company Training including practising the Attack, was carried out on "B" Area at 51c S.E R 10, 11, 12. Specialist classes in the afternoon	
	6th		The Battalion went for a Route March along the ARRAS — ST POL Road returning by the same route. Lewis Gunners fired on the MOAT RANGE; also "indifferent shots".	
	7th		The Field Firing Practise carried out by half Battalions on the 4th inst was repeated by the Battalion as a whole again under the inspection of the Divisional G.S.O 1.	
	8th		Training in "B" Area in the morning. The Commanding Officer and the Adjutant reconnoitred the portion of line in the MONCHY Sector held by the Left Battn. of the Right Brigade, which the Battn was due to	[illegible initials]

A7092 Wt. W123 9/M1293 750,000. 1/17. D. D & L. Ltd. Forms/C.2118/14.

Army Form C. 2118.

Instructions regarding War Diaries and Intelligence Summaries are contained in F. S. Regs., Part II. and the Staff Manual respectively. Title pages will be prepared in manuscript.

WAR DIARY
or
INTELLIGENCE SUMMARY.
(Erase heading not required.)

Place	Date	Hour	Summary of Events and Information	Remarks and references to Appendices
COLLEGE COMMUNALE ARRAS	8th (cont)		take over from the 1st Rifle Brigade on Dec 10th	
			Football in the afternoon against the 1st Royal Warwickshire Regt. the match was lost 0 — 4	
			Working and Carrying Parties were supplied to the Reserve Area.	
	9th		The 4 Coy Commanders the M.O and the Assistant Adjutant went to reconnoitre the new sector to be taken over on the morrow	
			C. of E., Non-conformist and Roman Catholic services were held	
Right sub-sector 10th Bde front E. of MONCHY LE-PREUX	10th		Battalion relieved 1st Bn. RIFLE BRIGADE (11th Inf Bde) in right sub-sector of 10th Inf Brigade front. Strength of Battalion in the line 13 officers & 486 O.R. No. 1 Coy. left front, No. 2 Coy right front, No. 3 Support, No. 4 Reserve. Battalion H.Q. in CURB SWITCH RESERVE. Battalion left COLLEGE COMMUNALE at 3 P.M. Relief complete at 9 P.M. On the way up the Battalion suffered 5 Casualties from shell fire including No 763 C of H BURROWS R.C. (died of wounds).	

Ruf [illegible]

A7092. Wt. 11128 9/M1293 750,000. 1/17. D. D & L. Ltd. Forms C2118/14.

Instructions regarding War Diaries and Intelligence Summaries are contained in F. S. Regs., Part II. and the Staff Manual respectively. Title pages will be prepared in manuscript.

WAR DIARY
or
INTELLIGENCE SUMMARY.
(Erase heading not required.)

Army Form C. 2118.

Place	Date	Hour	Summary of Events and Information	Remarks and references to Appendices
FRONT LINE E. of MONCHY LE PREUX.	11th		Trenches very wet & muddy, especially left subsector. Trench pumps manned throughout the day. A patrol went out from each front line company under 2/Lieut S.A. Rogers (No. 1 Coy.) and 2/Lieut C.F.P. Clewlow (No 2 Coy.) 2nd Lieut Rogers slightly wounded remained at duty	
	12th		At 4 A.M. 2/Lieut C.F.P. Clewlow, C. of H. Newman & 12 O.R left our front line at Sap 12 with the object of raiding the enemy's line to obtain identification. The night was rather light and the enemy was thoroughly on the alert. Heavy rifle & machine gun was opened on the party which after proceeding half across NO MAN'S LAND was forced to withdraw. C of H Newman was seriously wounded. At 4.20 a.m another attempt was made further South with the same result, the enemy manning his parapet. An inter Company relief was effected in the evening. No 4 Coy relieved No 1 Company. No 3 Coy relieved No 2 Coy.	
	13th		2nd Lieut. T.P.T. Burrowes & 3 O.R patrolled NO MAN'S LAND at night. Enemy was on the alert but showed no abnormal movement. 100 yards of wire put out in front of the front line by No 4 Coy	
	14th		8.15 a.m. Enemy Trench Mortars active on HIGHLAND SUPPORT. No 754 L/Cpl HIGGINS & 2 men of his L.G. team killed. Battalion was relieved in daylight by 2nd SEAFORTH HIGHLANDERS	[illegible signature]

Instructions regarding War Diaries and Intelligence Summaries are contained in F. S. Regs., Part II. and the Staff Manual respectively. Title pages will be prepared in manuscript.

WAR DIARY
or
INTELLIGENCE SUMMARY.
(Erase heading not required.)

Army Form C. 2118.

Place	Date	Hour	Summary of Events and Information	Remarks and references to Appendices
MONCHY DEFENCES	14th		Relief complete at 3 P.M. On relief Battalion moved into MONCHY DEFENCES. Battn H.Q in CIRCLE TRENCH just N. of its junction with CHERRY LANE. No. 1 Coy in Strong Points E G & H. No. 2 Coy in the BROWN LINE N. of ARRAS CAMBRAI road. No. 3 Coy in CIRCLE TR. No. 4 Coy in ORCHARD RESERVE. Severe frost set in.	
	15th		Working & carrying parties for front & support line & maintenance of Reserve line. 3 officers & 190 O.R.	
	16th		Working parties as above.	
	17th		" " " increased to 5 officers & 220 O.R.	
			Major N.W.S. CUNNINGHAME took over command of the Battalion from Lieut. Col. W.R. PORTAL D.S.O. proceeding on leave.	
Front line E of MONCHY	18th		Battalion relieved 2nd SEAFORTH HIGHLANDERS in right Sub-Sector. Distribution of sector altered on relief as follows – No 3 Coy in right sub-sector as before. No 4 Coy in left subsector with H.Q in SHAFT ALLEY. No 1 Company in support with Coy H.Q in HIGHLAND SUPPORT. No 2 in reserve in CIRCLE TR. Battalion H.Q in CIRCLE TR. Relief complete by 4.35 P.M.	
	19th		Severe frost has dried up the line considerably but owing to the hardness of the ground work became difficult	[illegible signature]

A7092 Wt. [illegible] D. D. & L. Ltd. Forms/C. 2118/[illegible]

Instructions regarding War Diaries and Intelligence Summaries are contained in F. S. Regs., Part II. and the Staff Manual respectively. Title pages will be prepared in manuscript.

WAR DIARY
or
INTELLIGENCE SUMMARY.
(Erase heading not required.)

Army Form C. 2118.

Place	Date	Hour	Summary of Events and Information	Remarks and references to Appendices
Front line E of MONCHY	19th		Patrols from both sub-sectors at night encountered no hostile patrols in No MAN'S LAND. Hostile working party in front of the right sub-sector dispersed by L.G. fire.	
	20th		Enemy shelled CANISTER & EAST RESERVE in the morning – otherwise quiet. Inter Company relief effected in the afternoon. No. 2 Coy relieved No 3 Coy. No. 1 Coy relieved No 4 Coy.	
	21st	5.15 P.M.	The enemy put down a heavy T.M. barrage on the front line N & S of Sap 12 completely blowing it in. At the same time an artillery barrage along the whole support line with 77 mm & 4.2 How, with 5.9 along CANISTER & EAST RESERVE. A raiding party of 30 to 40 of the enemy attempted to rush Sap 12. Rapid Lewis Gun & rifle fire was opened & only 5 Germans succeeded in getting to Sap. No 4401 L/Cpl DAVIES the N.C.O. i/c of the Sap immediately charged the raiders, who had seized one of our men, with the bayonet, killing one. The remainder escaped over a broken down piece of the trench. None of the garrison of the Sap were missing. The enemy barrage inflicted the following casualties among us – Killed. 2nd Lieut. J. W. BIRD (No 2 Coy) & 2 O.R. Wounded 10 O.R.	

Instructions regarding War Diaries and Intelligence Summaries are contained in F. S. Regs., Part II. and the Staff Manual respectively. Title pages will be prepared in manuscript.

WAR DIARY
or
INTELLIGENCE SUMMARY.
(Erase heading not required.)

Army Form C. 2118.

Place	Date	Hour	Summary of Events and Information	Remarks and references to Appendices
Front line E of MONCHY.	21st		1 identification obtained from dead German - 179th I.R. (normal). Lt Col. H.R. PORTAL returned from leave resumed command at 10 a.m. the day	
	22nd		Battalion was relieved by 2nd SEAFORTH HIGHLRS. Relief completed at 6.45 P.M. On relief Battalion moved to WILDERNESS CAMP where it was accommodated in NISSEN huts.	
WILDERNESS CAMP H31a93 (51B NW 1/20.000)	23rd		Carrying & working parties of 6 officers + 260 O.R. found at night for work in support & reserve lines under the R.E.	
	24th		Same parties found as on 23rd inst.	
	25th		Christmas Day. Working parties cancelled by Brigade. Christmas Service in Scottish Churches Tent at 10.0 a.m. Day of Rest.	
SCHRAMM BARRACKS ARRAS	26th		Working parties of 4 officers & 190 O.R. found at night. Battalion relieved by [illegible] Highlanders. Battalion moved to SCHRAMM BARRACKS, ARRAS at 3 P.M. with exception of working parties who rejoined later.	
	27th		Christmas day celebrated by the Battalion. Christmas dinners at 1 P.M. Turkey & plum puddings. Commanding Officer visited each Company & Headquarters Room during the dinner hour. Company concerts in the evening.	[signature]

Ayogo. Wt. [illegible] 750,000. 1/17. D. D. & L. Ltd. Forms/C. 2118/14.

Instructions regarding War Diaries and Intelligence Summaries are contained in F. S. Regs., Part II. and the Staff Manual respectively. Title pages will be prepared in manuscript.

WAR DIARY
or
INTELLIGENCE SUMMARY.
(Erase heading not required.)

Army Form C. 2118.

Place	Date	Hour	Summary of Events and Information	Remarks and references to Appendices
ECURAMM BARRACKS ARRAS	28th		Company training near BUTTE DE TIR. Hard frost continues. Party attached to N.Z.E.T.C. relieved by similar party. 1 N.C.O. & 30 men working at R.E. Dump.	
	29th		Company training. 1 N.C.O. & 30 men working at R.E. Dump.	
	30th		Permanent party of 1 N.C.O. & 20 men sent to work at R.E. Dump till 2nd prox. 5 N.C.O.s & 15 men detached for guard [illegible] till 2nd prox.	
WILDERNESS CAMP			Battalion relieved 2nd [illegible] Highlanders in WILDERNESS CAMP. Relief complete at 4.30 P.M.	
	31st		Company training. Working party of 1 officer & 35 O.R. found for [illegible]. Frost thoroughly set in for the last 17 days, together with [illegible] 6 inches of snow.	

R. [illegible]

A7092 Wt. W128 9/M1293 750,000. 1/17. D. D. & L. Ltd. Forms C2118/14.

4th Division

Household Battn.

Disbanded 15th Feb.

January – Part February

1918

Confidential

War Diary
of
Household Battalion
– from –
1st January 1918
– to –
31st January 1918

Volume 15

W. M. Baker Lt
for Lieut. Colonel
Commanding
Household Battalion

3/2/18

9W/15

Instructions regarding War Diaries and Intelligence Summaries are contained in F. S. Regs., Part II. and the Staff Manual respectively. Title pages will be prepared in manuscript.

WAR DIARY
or
INTELLIGENCE SUMMARY.
(Erase heading not required.)

Army Form C. 2118.

Place	Date	Hour	Summary of Events and Information	Remarks and references to Appendices
WILDERNESS CAMP H31 a 9 3 (SIGNW [illegible])	1st January 1918		Companies paraded for Company training. Improvements carried out on the huts which are in a bad & dilapidated condition. Major W.N.S. Cunningham took over command of 1st KING'S OWN (12th Brigade) at the end of last month & this was omitted from December War Diary.	
	2nd		Company training. Working party of 4 officers & 180 O.R. worked under R.E. [illegible] [illegible] line in vicinity of H36 d 1.5. Work [illegible] [illegible] by [illegible] of ground. 4 officers & 36 O.R. carrying were [illegible] line.	
	3rd		Battalion relieved 1st Battalion RIFLE BRIGADE in the right sub-sector of CAMBRAI road sector. Relief complete at 8.15 P.M. without casualty. No. 1 Coy on the right, No 3 on the left, No. 4 right support, No. 2 left support.	
	4th		Quiet day in line. Hard frost continues making work in trenches nearly impossible.	
	5th		Inter-Company relief. No. 4 relieved No 1 Coy. No 2 Coy relieved No 3 Coy. Light T.M. barrage put down by enemy in support line at 3.30 p.m. Wiring [illegible] in front of front line at night.	
	6th		Quiet day except for continued shelling of back areas.	R [illegible]

A7092 Wt. W123/9/M1293 750,000 1/17 D. D. & L. Ltd. Forms C2118/14

Army Form C. 2118.

Instructions regarding War Diaries and Intelligence Summaries are contained in F. S. Regs., Part II. and the Staff Manual respectively. Title pages will be prepared in manuscript.

WAR DIARY
or
INTELLIGENCE SUMMARY.
(Erase heading not required.)

Place	Date	Hour	Summary of Events and Information	Remarks and references to Appendices
CAMBRAI ROAD SECTOR.	7th		Battalion relieved by 2nd Seaforth Highlanders. On relief Battalion moved into Brigade Support. No. 1 Coy to SPADE RES. No 2 Coy to EAST RES., No. 3 Coy. to FORK RES., No 4 Coy to "E. D & E" Strong points. Battalion H-Q in LES FOSSES FARM. Relief complete by 3.35 P.M.	
Brigade Support Les Fosses Farm.	8th		No. 401 L/Cpl N DAVIES awarded D.C.M. for conspicuous gallantry in repelling enemy raid on the 21st ulto. Working parties of 70 O.R. found by day & night.	
	9th		Working parties as on 8th.	
	10th		Enemy shelled SPADE RESERVE with 4.2 Hows intermittently throughout the day.	
CAMBRAI ROAD SECTOR	11th		Battalion relieved the 2nd SEAFORTH HIGHLANDERS in the front line as Right Battalion of Left Brigade Sector. No 1 and 3 Coys to the Right and Left front respectively. No 2 Coy Left Support in SADDLE. No 4 Coy Right Support in HOB. Relief complete by 3.45 p.m. without casualties. A ~~patrol~~ listening patrol of 1 N.C.O. and 3 O.R. was sent out by No. 1 Coy.	

[illegible signature], Lt.

A7092 Wt. [illegible] 750,000 1/17 D. D. & L. Ltd. Forms/C.2118/14.

Army Form C. 2118.

Instructions regarding War Diaries and Intelligence Summaries are contained in F. S. Regs., Part II. and the Staff Manual respectively. Title pages will be prepared in manuscript.

WAR DIARY
or
INTELLIGENCE SUMMARY.
(Erase heading not required.)

Place	Date	Hour	Summary of Events and Information	Remarks and references to Appendices
	Jan 12th		Very quiet day. The front line trench was in good condition but the support trenches and parts of the communication trenches were very bad, through thaw. Parties working at the trenches were supplied by all Coys. and by Battn. H.Q.	
			2 Patrols were sent out, 1 each, from the Left and Right Front Coys. The Left Patrol located an enemy sap.	
	Jan 13th		At 4.50 a.m. the enemy put down a Trench Mortar and Artillery barrage on the front and support lines of the Battalion and of the 3/10 MIDDLESEX on our left. The barrage ended at 5.35 a.m. The MIDDLESEX sent up the S.O.S. signal and our M.Gs. T.Ms and artillery responded: the artillery only very lightly. The rest of the day was exceptionally quiet. The Bn. had 2 N.C.O.s of the Left Front Coy wounded.	
			Inter-company reliefs were carried out in the afternoon. No 2 Coy relieving No 3, and No 4 No 2 Coy. It was a day of brilliant visibility and a frost set in at night. 2 Wiring	Arthur Bamther Lt.

A7092. Wt. W128 9/M1293 750,000 1/17. D. D. & L., Ltd. Forms/C2118/14.

Instructions regarding War Diaries and Intelligence Summaries are contained in F. S. Regs., Part II. and the Staff Manual respectively. Title pages will be prepared in manuscript.

Army Form C. 2118.

WAR DIARY
or
INTELLIGENCE SUMMARY.
(Erase heading not required.)

Place	Date	Hour	Summary of Events and Information	Remarks and references to Appendices
	Jan 13 cont.		parties were sent out by each of the front line Coys. 2 Patrols were also sent out. No 4 Coy sent out 1 N.C.O. and 3 O.R. as a listening patrol on the left. 2nd Lieut A.H. DUFFEY took out 1 N.C.O. and 3 O.R. and bombed a M.G. in the Sap (located the previous evening). The patrol returned without being fired on and without casualties.	
	Jan 14.		Heavy snow fell in the morning and on this account no patrols were sent out. The day was very quiet. In the evening the 25th NORTHUMBERLAND FUSILIERS on our right had their wire cut by enemy T.M.s and a repairing party which they sent out was bombed back by the enemy.	
	Jan 15.		Very heavy thaw set in and our working parties including one from Battn. H.Q. could make no headway except the trenches which were falling. The well revetted front line alone held fairly good	[illegible] Lt.

A7092. Wt. W1238/M1293. 750,000. 1/17. D. D. & L. Ltd. Forms/C.2118/14.

Instructions regarding War Diaries and Intelligence Summaries are contained in F. S. Regs., Part II. and the Staff Manual respectively. Title pages will be prepared in manuscript.

WAR DIARY
or
INTELLIGENCE SUMMARY.
(*Erase heading not required.*)

Army Form C. 2118.

Place	Date	Hour	Summary of Events and Information	Remarks and references to Appendices
	Jan 15 cont.		Heavy rain fell in the afternoon. The SEAFORTH HIGHLANDERS in SUPPORT who were to relieve the HOUSEHOLD BATTALION, had first to be relieved by the 3/10 MIDDLESEX from the Left Front Line. The main communication trenches were nearly impassable, and made relieving very slow. Nos 1 3 and 4 Coys of the HOUSEHOLD BATTALION were clear by 11 pm, but No 2 Coy had to remain in the front line till 11 a.m. next morning. The Battalion moved into Brigade Reserve in the BROWN LINE. There were several casualties in the relief as the enemy shelled Pick the 'OUT' Trench heavily.	
BROWN LINE. Brigade RESERVE.	Jan 16		This day was spent by the Coys in collecting their men and getting clean. Heavy rain continued and made the quarters very bad. No working parties were supplied.	[illegible signature] Lt

A7092. Wt. W126 g/M1293. 750,000. 1/17. D. D. & L., Ltd. Forms/C2118/14.

Army Form C. 2118.

Instructions regarding War Diaries and Intelligence Summaries are contained in F. S. Regs., Part II. and the Staff Manual respectively. Title pages will be prepared in manuscript.

WAR DIARY
or
INTELLIGENCE SUMMARY.

(*Erase heading not required.*)

Place	Date	Hour	Summary of Events and Information	Remarks and references to Appendices
	Jan 17		Working parties of 2 half Companies by day and 2 half Companies by night engaged in digging out and revetting the main communication trenches.	
	Jan 18		ditto The Adjutant, Capt R W G Dixon M.C. went on leave.	
SCHRAMM BARRACKS, ARRAS	Jan 19		The 10th Infantry Brigade went into Reserve and the Battalion moved into the SCHRAMM BARRACKS ARRAS at 1 p.m.	
	Jan 20		No Church Parades. Inspection of billets in SCHRAMM BARRACKS by B.G.C. 10th Infy Bde at 11 a.m. Batt. bathed by Coys in the afternoon. A draft arrived from the Divn. Depot Camp of 37 O.R.	
	Jan 21.		Company Training and Shooting on the MOAT RANGE was interfered with by rain.	
	Jan 22		The Battalion went for a Route March, except No 4 Coy which was on a coal fatigue. Col. PORTAL M.V.O. D.S.O. proceeded on leave and Major FLEURY TEVANS, Second in Command took Command	[signature]

A7092 Wt. [illegible] 750,000 1/17 D.D.&L. Ltd. Forms/C. 2118/14.

Army Form C. 2118.

Instructions regarding War Diaries and Intelligence Summaries are contained in F. S. Regs., Part II. and the Staff Manual respectively. Title pages will be prepared in manuscript.

WAR DIARY
or
INTELLIGENCE SUMMARY.
(Erase heading not required.)

Place	Date	Hour	Summary of Events and Information	Remarks and references to Appendices
SCHRAMM BARRACKS ARRAS and WILDERNESS CAMP	Jan	23rd	The Battalion moved up in the morning to WILDERNESS CAMP relieving there the 2nd Seaforth Highlanders who moved down to ARRAS. Relief was complete by 1.0 p.m.	
			All available men from all 4 Companies went out on working parties under their Company Commanders in the evening, working on the Support Lines in the MONCHY Sector.	
			Two Platoons only instead of going on the working parties, practised an intended raid. The OC Raid was to be Lieut J A G Roberts with a Platoon from No 4 Coy; also Sec Lieut J P F BURCHELL with a Platoon from No 3 Coy. Capt H. WILLIAMSON superintended the raid practising.	
			On this occasion, no details were left in ARRAS; the whole Battalion moved up.	
	Jan	24.	Similar working parties supplied.	[illegible]

A7092. Wt. W 128 9/M1293 750,000 1/17. D. D. & L., Ltd. Forms C2118/14.

Army Form C. 2118.

WAR DIARY
or
INTELLIGENCE SUMMARY.
(Erase heading not required.)

Instructions regarding War Diaries and Intelligence Summaries are contained in F. S. Regs., Part II. and the Staff Manual respectively. Title pages will be prepared in manuscript.

Place	Date	Hour	Summary of Events and Information	Remarks and references to Appendices
Jan 24th 25			Same as on previous day. In the evening, Coy. Commanders went up to the 1st Rifle Brigade Right Battalion in the MONCHY Sector, and reconnoitred their new positions. They were accompanied by their Coy. Corporal Majors. The condition of the trenches, necessitated traffic along overland duck-board tracks, so a reconnaissance could only be made after dark.	
Jan 26th			On the eve of going into the front line all the Companies again supplied working parties of all their available strength. The C.O. and Adjutant went up in the morning to make arrangements for the relief with the 1st Rifle Brigade.	
Jan 27th Wilderness Camp and Front Line.			The Battalion relieved the 1st Rifle Bde as Right Battalion in the MONCHY Sector; the 10th Brigade now relieving the 12th Bde which went into Reserve. The Companies were distributed as follows:	[signature] Lt.

A7092 Wt. W128 9/M1293 750,000. 1/17. D. D. & L. Ltd. Forms/C2118/14.

WAR DIARY
or
INTELLIGENCE SUMMARY.
(Erase heading not required.)

Army Form C. 2118.

Instructions regarding War Diaries and Intelligence Summaries are contained in F. S. Regs., Part II. and the Staff Manual respectively. Title pages will be prepared in manuscript.

Place	Date	Hour	Summary of Events and Information	Remarks and references to Appendices
Jan 27th cont			No 1. Coy. — Left Front Coy No 2 Coy — Right Front Coy No 3 Coy — Reserve Coy. No 4 Coy — Support Coy. Battalion Headquarters were in CIRCLE TRENCH. Relief was complete by 8.10 p.m. Battalion strength. 18 officers and 424 O.R. This was to be the Household Battalions last tour in the line. Details consisting of the Band, the 2 Platoons selected for the Raid, ~~[illegible]~~ and about 150 O.R. returned to SCHRAMM BARRACKS ARRAS under the Command of Capt. F.R. DAKEYNE, the Transport Officer	
Jan. 28th			Communication with the front line was only possible across the top and therefore restricted to the hours between dusk and dawn. Evening Stand-to was at 4.30 p.m., morning Stand to at 6.10 a.m. 2 Patrols were sent out from No 1 Coy and 1 from No. 2 Coy. to patrol	[signature]

A7092. Wt. W.2809/M1293. 750,000. 1/17. D. D. & L., Ltd. Forms C2118/14.

Instructions regarding War Diaries and Intelligence Summaries are contained in F. S. Regs., Part II. and the Staff Manual respectively. Title pages will be prepared in manuscript.

WAR DIARY
or
INTELLIGENCE SUMMARY.
(*Erase heading not required.*)

Army Form C. 2118.

Place	Date	Hour	Summary of Events and Information	Remarks and references to Appendices
Jan 28. cont.			NO MANS LAND. The enemy was heard working in his front line	
Jan 29.			At 3 a.m a heavy barrage was put down by the enemy on the Left Front and Support Coys. No attack followed. Our artillery replied with a slow rate of fire. 1 O.R. was killed in No 4 Coy, and 3 O.R. wounded, 1 of these subsequently died of wounds.	
			From 7.30 – 8.30 a.m. another barrage was put down on the same frontage and No 1 Coy. suffered a direct hit on a Lewis Gun Post. 3 O.R. were killed and 1 wounded.	
			In the evening 3 N.C.Os and 25 O.R. were brought up from No 2 Coy. Details to assist the Reserve Coy – No 3 – in the work of carrying for the 2 front Coys. The Support Coy. carried for itself.	
			An advanced post was pushed out from dusk to dawn by the Left Front Coy. to act as a Standing Patrol.	
			Lieut R JEWITT (No 2. Coy) was wounded by a sniper in the afternoon.	[signature] Lt

A6092. Wt. W125 9 M293 750,000. 1/17. D. D. & L. Ltd. Forms/C2118/14.

Instructions regarding War Diaries and Intelligence Summaries are contained in F. S. Regs., Part II. and the Staff Manual respectively. Title pages will be prepared in manuscript.

WAR DIARY
or
INTELLIGENCE SUMMARY.
(Erase heading not required.)

Army Form C. 2118.

Place	Date	Hour	Summary of Events and Information	Remarks and references to Appendices
Jan 30th			Inter-Company reliefs were carried out after dusk, and completed almost simultaneously by 8.30 pm No 1 Coy became ~~Reserve~~ Support Coy. 2 " Reserve " 3 " Right Front Coy 4 " Left Front Coy No 4 Coy. sent out 2 advanced posts and 1 patrol at dusk; No 3 Coy. 1 patrol at dawn. The artillery on both sides were active.	
Jan 31st			A very misty day and movement overland as far as the Support Line involved no danger. The Right Front Coy was trench-mortared in the early afternoon. A party of Officers and N.C.O.s from the 10th Argyll and Sutherland Highlanders from the 15th Division came up in the morning to reconnoitre the Sector. In the evening, Coy Cdrs from the 2nd Seaforth Highlanders came to arrange details of the morrows relief with their opposite numbers.	Wm Butler Lt

A7092. Wt. W128 9/M1293 750,000. 1/17. D. D & L. Ltd. Forms/C2118/14.

Confidential

War Diary

— of —

Household Battalion

— from —

1st February 1918.

— until —

date of Disbandment
15th February 1918

Volume 16.

15/2/18

H. J. Thomas.
Lieut & Adjt
Household Battn.

16

Army Form C. 2118.

Instructions regarding War Diaries and Intelligence Summaries are contained in F. S. Regs., Part II. and the Staff Manual respectively. Title pages will be prepared in manuscript.

WAR DIARY
or
INTELLIGENCE SUMMARY.
(Erase heading not required.)

Place	Date	Hour	Summary of Events and Information	Remarks and references to Appendices
Right Front Battalion in MONCHY Sector – CIRCLE TRENCH – and Support Battn in CURB SWITCH SOUTH.	Feb 1		Like the previous day this day was very misty and it was safe to walk overland anywhere except up to the Front Line. The day was also very quiet. The Battalion was relieved by the 2nd Seaforth Highlanders and became Support Battalion in the MONCHY SECTOR No 1 Coy went to CURB SWITCH SOUTH 2 to Strong Points 'F' 'G' and 'H' Coy HQ at 'F' 3 to ORCHARD TRENCH 4 to MUSKET TRENCH. Battn HQ CURB SWITCH. Relief was complete by 8.5 p.m. This last tour of the Battalion in the front line was made very complicated by the impassibility of the communication trenches. Both front Coys. wore gum-boots the whole time and socks were changed every 24 hours and sent down to ARRAS to be dried. The 2 front Coys sent back before dawn to their Cookhouses for hot tea which was in petrol tins packed with hay into packs. This kept the tea warm satisfactorily.	Arthur Battye Lt.

A7092. Wt. W128 9/M1293 750,000 1/17 D. D & L. Ltd. Forms/C2118/14

Instructions regarding War Diaries and Intelligence Summaries are contained in F. S. Regs., Part II. and the Staff Manual respectively. Title pages will be prepared in manuscript.

WAR DIARY
or
INTELLIGENCE SUMMARY.
(Erase heading not required.)

Army Form C. 2118.

Place	Date	Hour	Summary of Events and Information	Remarks and references to Appendices
Feb 1 cont.			The enemy's trenches were, according to prisoners' accounts in a worse condition than our own, and he was constantly at work on them. Many working parties and one attempt to fraternise by waving a handkerchief, were dispersed by our Lewis Gun fire.	
			From 10.30 till 10.55 p.m. after Relief was complete, the enemy put down a heavy barrage on our late left front Coy. sector, and immediately north of it. Our guns fired on S.O.S lines. Enemy M Gs and a few guns fired on CORBS SWITCH. 25 III O.R. from No 2 Coy sent down to Details	No 2 Coy Details
Feb 2.			Our guns put on a barrage on the CAMBRAI ROAD SECTOR at 8 a.m. to protect a successful daylight raid carried out by West Riding troops.	
			9 groups were supplied by Nos. 1, 3 and 4 Coys, working after dark on support lines and Communication trenches.	
			10 men from each of these Coys were sent down to ARRAS and a similar number of fresh men came up from Details.	
Feb 3rd			ditto. A few gas shells fell on CORBS SWITCH at 10 p.m. Lieut Col. PORTAL M.V.O. D.S.O. and Captain DILL M.C. returned from leave to Details and Bde HQ respectively.	[illegible] Lt.

A7092 Wt. W2325/M1295 750,000 1/17. D. D. & L. Ltd. Forms/C2118/14

Instructions regarding War Diaries and Intelligence Summaries are contained in F. S. Regs., Part II. and the Staff Manual respectively. Title pages will be prepared in manuscript.

WAR DIARY
or
INTELLIGENCE SUMMARY.

(Erase heading not required.)

Army Form C. 2118.

Place	Date	Hour	Summary of Events and Information	Remarks and references to Appendices
Feb	4th		Same working parties : 26 men sent down to Details and 26 brought up.	
Feb	5th.		Same working parties Day very quiet.	
Feb	6th		4th Division went into rest The Battalion was relieved by 3 different units of the 15th Division. No 1 Coy was relieved by 6th Cameron Highlanders. 2 by Royal Scots Fusiliers 3 by 11th Argyll and Sutherland Highlanders. 4 by 6th Cameron Highlanders Battalion HQ by 6th Cameron Highlanders Relief was complete by 11 30 pm. The Battalion marched down to the Maison Rouge on the ARRAS – CAMBRAI road, and was thence conveyed by train to ARRAS; the last Coy. arriving in ARRAS – COLLEGE COMMUNAL at 1.30 a.m. on the following day. The Batt. while 5 days in Support had 1 O.R. wounded	[illegible] Lt.

A7092. Wt. W125 g/M1293. 750,000. 1/17. D. D. & L. Ltd. Forms/C2118/14.

Instructions regarding War Diaries and Intelligence Summaries are contained in F. S. Regs., Part II. and the Staff Manual respectively. Title pages will be prepared in manuscript.

WAR DIARY
or
INTELLIGENCE SUMMARY.
(Erase heading not required.)

Army Form C. 2118.

Place	Date	Hour	Summary of Events and Information	Remarks and references to Appendices
COLLEGE COMMUNALE	7th		Final orders regarding disbandment of the Battalion received	
ARRAS	8th		Day spent in cleaning up and handing over kit. H.M. the King's Farewell Order read out on Parade to the whole Battalion.	
	9th		Battalion paraded at 8.30 a.m. & marched to Parade Ground South of BUTTE DE TIR. Major-General T.G. MATHESON C.B. Commanding 4th Division inspected the Battalion. The Battalion marched past in column of platoons. The G.O.C. then addressed the Battalion & bade them farewell.	
	10th		Disbandment	
			1. All duration men paraded at 9.30 a.m. and marched to XVII Corps M & R Camp AGNEZ-LES-DUISANS for transfer to the Foot Guards under Lts. E.N. de GEIJER, J.S. ELLIS, J.A.G. ROBERTS, A.W. BRAWN & 2nd Lts. J.P.T. BURCHELL, C.D. WHITEHOUSE & P.Y. BELLY	
			2. 46 candidates for temporary commissions in the Infantry paraded at 2 P.M. & marched to 4th Div. Depot Batt. DUISANS for transfer to ENGLAND.	
			3. Lts. A.R. GILBEY & T.H. SANDFORD & 41 serving soldiers paraded at 4.0 P.M. & proceeded by train to ROUEN to rejoin their original regiments	

A7092 Wt. W148 9/M1293 750,000 1/17 D. D. & L. Ltd. Forms C2118/14

Instructions regarding War Diaries and Intelligence Summaries are contained in F. S. Regs., Part II. and the Staff Manual respectively. Title pages will be prepared in manuscript.

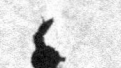

WAR DIARY
or
INTELLIGENCE SUMMARY.
(*Erase heading not required.*)

Army Form C. 2118.

Place	Date	Hour	Summary of Events and Information	Remarks and references to Appendices
ARRAS	11th			
	12th		Battalion H Q only left in ARRAS	
	13th			
	14th			
	15th		Battalion H Q disbanded	

(A7092). Wt. W12839/M1293. 750,000. 1/17. D. D. & L., Ltd. Forms/C.2118/14.

www.ingramcontent.com/pod-product-compliance
Lightning Source LLC
Chambersburg PA
CBHW080907230426
43664CB00016B/2744